All things are possible to him who believes.
Jesus Christ
Mark 9:23

Believing God
for the Impossible

Books and booklets by Bill Bright

Come Help Change Our World
Believing God for the Impossible
A Movement of Miracles
Revolution Now!
Ten Basic Steps Toward Christian Maturity
How to Be Sure You Are a Christian
How to Experience God's Love and Forgiveness
How to Walk in the Spirit
How to Witness in the Spirit
How to Be Filled With the Spirit
How to Introduce Others to Christ
How to Love by Faith
How to Pray
How to Help Fulfill the Great Commission
Have You Heard of the Four Spiritual Laws?
Have You Made the Wonderful Discovery of the
   Spirit-filled Life?
Jesus and the Intellectual
Your Duties as a Christian Citizen
Paul Brown Letter
Van Dusen Letter

Believing God for the Impossible

A CALL TO SUPERNATURAL LIVING

Bill Bright

CAMPUS CRUSADE FOR CHRIST INTERNATIONAL
San Bernardino, California 92414

Dedication

Dedicated to my beloved wife, Vonette, who has believed God for the impossible with me for more than 30 years. Without her love and encouragement, prayers and full cooperation, I probably would never have experienced or written about *Believing God for the Impossible – A Call to Supernatural Living.*

All things are possible to him who believes.
Jesus Christ
Mark 9:23

Table of Contents

Preface

Of all the people whom I have known throughout the world, the one person whose life has most effectively and consistently demonstrated a supernatural quality is my mother, who is 89 years old. She has walked with our Master, her dearest friend, since she received Him as her Savior and Lord at the age of 16. At that time she promised to obey and serve her Lord wherever He might lead and whatever He might ask her to do.

My mother dedicated me to Christ before I was born, and her prayers have followed me every day of my life. From my earliest remembrance, she began every day and ended every day reading her Bible and praying. I have pleasant memories of my mother singing softly many Christian hymns of worship and praise as she cooked and sewed, cleaned house and cared for the needs of a family of seven children.

It is possible that I could be accused of prejudice and forgetfulness, but try as I might, I do not remember a single time when I heard or saw my mother say or do anything that violated the commitment which she made to her Lord and mine almost 75 years ago.

This poem was recently written by my mother:

I need Jesus every morning
As the day breaks o'er the land
And I thank Him for a peaceful rest
And for His guiding hand.
I need Him at the noontide hour
When all seems bright and fair
I praise Him for His boundless love
And His presence everywhere.

I need Him at the eventide
When day fades into night.
I thank Him that I know
He is my eternal light.
Oh, I find that I need Jesus
Every hour of every day
He is my refuge and strength
The life, the truth, the way.

He is my Rock of Ages
My shelter from life's storms
My good shepherd who watches o'er me
And keeps me from all harm.
With the Holy Spirit to guide me
I can make my life sublime
I'm glad He knows my future
In His hands, He holds my time.

Just to be alone with Jesus
Just to know how much He cares
Gives this life a bit of Eden
That I want the world to share.
Just to claim His precious promises
As I walk and talk with Him here
Gives a sweet foretaste of heaven
In a world so fraught with fear.

— Mary Lee Bright

This poem reveals the secret of my mother's supernatural life-style and the reason that she believes God for the impossible.

Bill Bright

Acknowledgements

I would like to gratefully acknowledge Pat Means for his counsel on this manuscript at its beginning stages.

Also, I would like to express my sincere thanks to Sharon Fischer for her investment of many hours of research, and for her fine editorial assistance in the refinement of the manuscript. My thanks also to Tom Barton for the role he played in this regard.

Finally, my gratitude goes to Janet Kobobel and Erma Griswold for their excellent contribution in the final editing of this book, and to Frank Allnut and the Here's Life Publishers staff for overseeing its production.

Introduction

So You Are Born Again – Then Live Like It! was the working title of this book when I first started writing it more than two years ago. But that title seemed a bit too judgmental so I changed it to *So You Are Born Again – Here's How to Live Like It.*

The scriptural expression "born again" had become popular prior to the 1976 presidential election when the two major candidates, Gerald Ford and Jimmy Carter, identified themselves as "born again Christians" and Chuck Colson wrote his famous best-selling autobiography *Born Again.*

There was so much talk about born again Christianity that the Gallup poll conducted a survey. To most everyone's surprise, the results indicated that in 1976 there were approximately 50 million persons in the United States above the age of 18 who claimed they had been born again. On the basis of our experience of working with hundreds of thousands of students, I believe it is reasonable to assume that there are 25 million more below the age of 18 who would also identify themselves as born again.

On the surface, this is cause for great rejoicing, until one begins to ask, "Where are all those Christians?" There seems to be little evidence of their influence in any major facet of society: the home, education, government, media, entertainment, capital, labor, the professions. Jesus commanded His disciples to be the "salt of the earth" and the "light of the world."[1]

But where are those who are the "salt" and "light"? Why do professing Christians who number approximately 130 million Protestants and Catholics, including those who profess to be "born again," make so little impact for good in our society? Why does crime continue to skyrocket, homes continue to disintegrate, pornographic films, television and literature continue to inundate the land with the filth of depraved minds? Why has our educational system, once Christian, conceived with a biblical basis and born in the church, rejected Christ and adopted the false religion of secular humanism?

I believe there is a good reason for this: Most of those who profess to be Christians, followers of Christ, do not *live* like followers of Christ.

J. B. Phillips in his introduction to his translation of the New Testament Epistles, *Letters to Young Churches,* speaks directly to this issue. He writes, "The great difference between present-day Christianity and that of which we read in these letters is that to us it is primarily a performance; to them it was a real experience. We are apt to reduce the Christian religion to a code, or at best a rule of heart and life. To these men it is quite plainly the invasion of their lives by a new quality of life altogether. They do not hesitate to describe this as Christ 'living in' them. . . . Perhaps if we believed what they believed, we might achieve what they achieved."[2]

Because it is my desire to see the church of Jesus Christ infused again with this "new quality of life," I have again chosen a different title — *Believing God for the Impossible: A Call to Supernatural Living.* I have written this book with certain thoughts in mind. First, most Christians freely, but sadly, admit that they are living defeated, frustrated and spiritually fruitless lives.

Second, most Christians are not happy with their present state. Third, defeated Christians do not need to be criticized, condemned, ridiculed and "put down." They are already plagued with guilt and defeat.

Fourth, they need to be loved, understood and helped to experience the full, rich and abundant life which Jesus promised to all who walk in faith and obedience to Him and His teachings.

Fifth, most Christians will gladly and joyfully respond to a clear, understandable, scriptural explanation of how to live the Christian life as Jesus meant for us to live it. The truths emphasized in this book have influenced the lives of millions of people around the world for Christ.

I commend the message of this book to you, dear reader, with the earnest prayer that your life, too, will be enriched, blessed, even transformed by the love and power of God as you read, and that you will be impressed by Him to share these truths with your loved ones and friends.

Bill Bright
Arrowhead Springs

CHAPTER ONE

A Supernatural View of God

The Christian life is an exciting, joy-filled adventure! Never before have I felt this more strongly or experienced this truth more fully than today, after more than 30 years of walking with our Lord.

Jesus promised the full and abundant life for all those who walk in faith and obedience. "I came that they might have life, and might have it abundantly."[1] ". . . He who believes in Me, the works that I do shall he do also, and greater than these shall he do, because I go to the Father."[2] "If you ask anything in My name, I will do it."[3]

But most Christians do not live joyful and fruitful lives. Why? Because they have a *limited view of God*. I am convinced that no one can ever begin to live supernaturally and have the faith to believe God for impossible things, if he does not know what God is like, or if he harbors misunderstandings about God and His character.

Would you like to live a joyful, abundant and fruitful life — every day filled with adventure? You can!

Get to Know God

You start by getting to know God, who He is, what He is like, and the benefits which we enjoy when we belong to Him. Your view of God influences all of the rest of your relationships. The Bible says that the just shall live by faith. Faith must have an object and the object of our faith is God.

Our view of God determines the quality of our faith. A small view of God results in a small faith. But great faith is the result of a correct biblical view of God as one who is great and worthy of our trust!

Our view of God as sovereign, holy, loving, righteous, just and compassionate produces these same qualities in our lives. For example, our view of God as a God of love and forgiveness prompts us to be loving and forgiving toward others.

What is God like to you? Is He a divine Santa Claus, a cosmic policeman, a dictator or a big bully? Many have distorted views of God and as a result are afraid of Him because they do not know what He is really like. Our heavenly Father yearns for us to respond to His love. It is only as we respond to that which we know to be true of God according to Scripture that we are able to come joyfully into His presence and know the adventure for which He created us.

The Most Important Thing

A. W. Tozer in his book *The Knowledge of the Holy* says, "What comes into our minds when we think about God is the most important thing about us. The history of mankind will probably show that no people has ever risen above its religion, and man's spiritual history will positively demonstrate that no religion has ever been greater than its idea of God. For this reason the gravest question before the Church is always God Himself, and the most portentous fact about any man is not what he at any given time may say or do, but what he in his deep heart conceives God to be like. We tend by a secret law of the soul to move toward our mental image of God.

"Were we able to extract from any man a complete answer to the question, 'What comes into your mind when you think about God?' we might predict with certainty the spiritual future of that man."[4]

Daniel Webster, who is recognized as one of the greatest intellects in American history, was asked, "What is the most important thought your mind has ever entertained?" He replied, "My accountability to God." Webster possessed an exalted view of God which he had gained from a life-long study of the Bible. His view of God had influenced his illustrious and noble contribution to the good of mankind.

Dr. William Lyon Phelps, one of Yale University's most distinguished professors, said, "I would rather have a thorough knowledge of the Scriptures than a college education." His knowledge of Scripture enhanced his view of God and thus influenced his life as a great scholar.

King David had the right perspective of God. His God was the infinite God of the universe. He writes in Psalms 139, "Where can I go from Thy Spirit? Or where can I flee from Thy presence? If I ascend to heaven, Thou art there; if I make my bed in Sheol, behold, Thou art there. If I take the wings of the dawn, if I dwell in the remotest part of the sea, even there Thy hand will lead me, and Thy right hand will lay hold of me."[5]

Praise to Our God and King!

Again in Psalms 145:1-7 David expresses his view of God, "I will praise You, my God and King, and bless Your name each day and forever. Great is Jehovah! Greatly praise Him! Let each generation tell its children what glorious things He does. I will meditate about Your glory, splendor, majesty and miracles. Your awe-inspiring deeds shall be on every tongue; I will proclaim Your greatness. Everyone will tell about how good You are, and sing about Your righteousness. . . ."

Some time ago, I found it necessary to fly from Los Angeles to New York, and after only three hours in New York to fly to Portland, Ore., to speak to several hundred pastors at a pastor's conference.

I was bone tired. Every fiber of my being ached with fatigue, as I waited for my luggage in the Portland airport. In only 30 minutes I would be speaking to the pastors. As I stood in the terminal, I felt impressed to pray, "Lord, do You have something that You would like to share with me?"

I immediately felt another impression — to turn to the 40th chapter of Isaiah, and I began to read a familiar passage which at the moment had new and current meaning. "Don't you know by now, that the everlasting God, the creator of the farthest parts of the earth, never grows faint or weary. . . . No one can fathom the depths of His understanding. He gives power to the tired and worn out. And strength to the weak." Certainly I could identify with the writer, for I was tired and absolutely worn out.

I continued to read, "Even the youths shall be exhausted, and the young men will all give up. But they that wait upon the Lord shall renew their strength. They shall mount up with wings like eagles; they shall run and not be weary; they shall walk and not faint."[6] At that moment, it was as though a great infusion of power flooded my very being. I was so excited as I contemplated who God is that I felt I could have thrown my luggage over the building and run to the meeting some miles away.

Rapid Transformation

Suddenly, I could hardly wait to stand before those servants of God and proclaim to them the wonders and majesty, the glory and power, the faithfulness of our God. Within 30 minutes or so, I did have that privilege, and God empowered and anointed me for the occasion in a marvelous way. Yes, a right understanding of who God is and of all the benefits we enjoy because we belong to Him will revolutionize the life of any and every believer and launch him into the exciting adventure of supernatural living.

A proper understanding of God's attributes will also open us up to the joy of "delighting in the Lord." In Psalms 37:4 we are promised, "Delight yourself in the Lord, and He will give you the desires of your heart." In other words, to live a full, exciting, adventuresome life, learn to delight yourself in the Lord.

How do we "delight" in Him? The first psalm gives us some idea of what that means. "Oh, the joys of those who do not follow evil men's advice, who do not hang around with sinners, scoffing at the things of God. But," and note these three things, "they delight in doing everything God wants them to, and day and night are always meditating on His laws and thinking about ways to follow Him more closely.

A Prosperous Life

"They are like trees along a river bank bearing luscious fruit each season without fail. Their leaves shall never wither, and all they do shall prosper.

"But for sinners, what a different story! They blow away like chaff before the wind. They are not safe on Judgment Day; they shall not stand among the godly.

"For the Lord watches over all the plans and paths of godly men, but the paths of the godless lead to doom."[7]

The successful, fruitful, joyful Christian life is one that is filled with thoughts which are focused on our wonderful God and His attributes, getting to know Him better as we seek His face.

Seeking God

What does it mean to "seek" God's face? In II Chronicles 7:14 we are admonished through a promise God gave to Solomon, "If . . . My people who are called by My name humble themselves and pray, and *seek My face* [italics mine] and turn from their wicked ways, then I will hear from heaven, will forgive their sin and will heal their land."

For years, I have quoted II Chronicles 7:14, and my emphasis in using the verse has been on the humbling of ourselves and turning from sin. But recently, a minister friend made a passing reference to the phrase, "seeking God's face," and it triggered in my mind some new thoughts about the verse.

For, in a sense, the humbling of ourselves and turning from sin are the by-products, or end results, of coming to know God as He is, by meditating upon His character and attributes. To seek God's face is to meditate upon His sovereignty, His holiness, His power, His wisdom, His love . . . getting to know *Him* as He is.

Exalted View

The disciples of the first-century church certainly had an exalted view of God. They prayed in Acts 4, "O Lord, Creator of heaven and earth and of the sea and everything in them — You spoke long ago by the Holy Spirit through our ancestor King David, your servant, saying, 'Why do the heathen rage against the Lord, and the foolish nations plan their little plots against Almighty God? The kings of the earth unite to fight against Him, and against the anointed Son of God!'

"That is what is happening here in this city today! For Herod the king, and Pontius Pilate the governor, and all the Romans — as well as the people of Israel — are united against Jesus, Your anointed Son, Your holy servant. *They won't stop at anything that You in Your wise power will let them do* . . ."[8] [italics mine].

Their God could do anything. There was nothing too great for Him. And the church today can once again experience that same dynamic which characterized those first believers, if we, too, become totally absorbed in the character and attributes of our great God. It is then that we will truly begin to believe God for supernatural, impossible things and make an impact for good on the world unlike any time in the history of man.

CHAPTER TWO

Jesus: The Source of the Supernatural Life

More than 30 years ago as a new Christian I read a statement concerning Jesus Christ that has had a profound influence on my life and ministry. Professor James Stewart, the late, famous New Testament scholar of Edinburgh, Scotland, proclaimed in his book entitled *The Strong Name:* "If we could but show the world that being committed to Christ is no tame, humdrum, sheltered monotony — but the most exciting adventure the human spirit can ever know, those who have been standing outside the Church and looking askance at Christ will come crowding in to pay allegiance, and we may well expect the greatest spiritual revival since Pentecost."[1]

I believed that statement to be true then, but now after these many exciting and incredibly adventuresome years of knowing and serving Jesus Christ, I am more convinced than ever of its accuracy.

All through my years as a student, as a college professor, and as a young businessman, I was an agnostic. In reality, I was a biblical and spiritual illiterate. I knew almost nothing about God, Jesus Christ, the Bible or the Christian faith — a fact which I have discovered is true of most students, professors and leaders of our nation and the world today.

Everyone Must Know

Through a series of experiences, which I shall explain later, I began to study the life and influence of Jesus of Nazareth in Scripture and in history. As a result, I received Him as my Savior and Lord. Later I did graduate work at Princeton and Fuller Theological Seminaries, where I studied under several internationally-known theologians.

The more I have learned about Jesus Christ, the more excited I have become about Him, and the more convinced I am that everyone needs to know Him and to experience His love and forgiveness.

From my own personal experience working with the staff of Campus Crusade for Christ — a ministry which is helping to touch the lives of millions throughout the world — I am convinced that literally hundreds of millions now living would receive Jesus Christ as their Savior and follow Him as their Lord if only they could know the truth about Him — who He is and why He came to this earth. They could not help but want to experience the rich, personal benefits which come to all who follow Him in faith and obedience, if only they knew about Him and how to receive Him.

An anonymous writer has described the world-changing influence of Jesus as follows: "All the armies that ever marched and all the navies that were ever built, and all the parliaments that ever sat, and all the kings that have ever reigned, put together have not affected the life of man upon this earth as has that *one solitary life!*" [italics mine].

On every continent and in scores of countries for more than 25 years, I have asked thousands of people, including Muslims, Hindus, Buddhists, communists and atheists: "Who is the greatest person who ever lived? Who has done more good for mankind than anyone else?" The answer is always the same — "Jesus of Nazareth."

Some time ago, I visited a famous university where I met with the leader of a radical student movement — one who was born into another religion, a professed atheist and an avowed communist. I asked this person the same question I had asked so many others.

There was a long, awkward silence and finally this reluctant reply: "I guess I would have to say Jesus of Nazareth."

Who He Is

Jesus of Nazareth was born nearly 2,000 years ago. For centuries the great prophets of Israel had foretold His coming. The Old Testament, which was written by many individuals over a period of 1,500 years, contains more than 300 references concerning the promised Messiah. All of these prophecies have been fulfilled in the birth, life, ministry, death and resurrection of Jesus. They could not have been speaking about anyone else.

That in itself is conclusive evidence of God's personal and supernatural intervention in history. Jesus' coming into this world was no accident. Neither was it a mystery, for according to Scripture, "Long ago, even before He made the world, God chose us to be His very own, through what Christ would do for us; He decided then to make us holy in His eyes, without a single fault — we who stand before Him covered with His love."[2]

In each book containing prophecy in the Old Testament, predictions of the coming King are made. Every generation from Isaiah onward bore witness to this supernatural promise of God. That is why for hundreds of years the scholars of Israel looked forward to the coming of their Messiah.

For example, over 400 years before Jesus' birth, the prophet Micah foretold the precise location of that event: "O Bethlehem Ephrathah, you are but a small Judean village, yet you will be the birthplace of my King who is alive from everlasting ages past!"[3]

Thus, when King Herod inquired of the priests and scribes where the Messiah was to be born, they replied, "In Bethlehem of Judea: for thus it is written by the prophet, 'And thou Bethlehem, in the land of Judah, art not the least among the princes of Judah; for out of thee shall come a Governor, that shall rule My people Israel.' "[4]

Plan Revealed

God's Word further records the supernatural role of Jesus Christ in history: "Long ago God spoke in many different ways to our fathers through the prophets (in visions, dreams, and even face to face), telling them little by little about His plans.

"But now in these days He has spoken to us through His Son to whom He has given everything, and through whom He made the world and everything there is.

"God's Son shines out with God's glory, and all that God's Son is and does marks Him as God. He regulates the universe by the mighty power of His command. He is the one who died to cleanse us and clear our record of all sin, and then sat down in highest honor beside the great God of heaven."[5]

Through the centuries man has demanded signs which would enable him to discern what is true. God promised that the people could know when the true Son of God had appeared: ". . . The Lord Himself will choose the sign — a child shall be born to a virgin! And she shall call Him Immanuel (meaning, 'God is with us')."[6]

In making his written report concerning the life of Jesus, Matthew emphasized the supernatural manner by which Christ entered into human life through a virgin birth. This supernatural birth set the stage for His perfect life of righteousness before God and man: "These are the facts concerning the birth of Jesus Christ: His mother, Mary, was engaged to be married to Joseph. But while she was still a virgin she became pregnant by the Holy Spirit. Then Joseph, her fiancé, being a man of stern principle, decided to break the engagement but to do it quietly, as he didn't want to publicly disgrace her.

"As he lay awake considering this, he fell into a dream, and saw an angel standing beside him. 'Joseph, son of David,' the angel said, 'don't hesitate to take Mary as your wife! For the child within her has been conceived by the Holy Spirit. And she will have a Son, and you shall name Him Jesus (meaning "Savior"), for He will save His people from their sins. This will fulfill God's message through His prophets — *Listen! The virgin shall conceive a child!* She shall give birth to a Son, and He shall be called 'Emmanuel' (meaning 'God is with us')." '

"When Joseph awoke, he did as the angel commanded, and brought Mary home to be his wife, but she remained a virgin until her Son was born; and Joseph named Him 'Jesus.' "[7]

Ultimate Expression

Although nearly 2,000 years have passed since He walked this earth, Jesus still stands as the ultimate expression of ethics and morality. Whatever one might think about Christians or the church, there are no blemishes in the character of Jesus.

God's Word, as recorded in the book of Hebrews, tells us, Jesus ". . . had the same temptations we do, though He never once gave way to them and sinned."[8] Our Lord thus stands out as the supreme example of one who practiced the things that He taught others and that He expects of His followers.

We today still stand in the almighty shadow of God's omnipotent promise: "For God has allowed us to know the secret of His plan, and it is this: He purposes in His sovereign will that all human history shall be consummated in Christ, that everything that exists in Heaven or earth shall find its perfection and fulfillment in Him."[9]

Perhaps the greatest testimony that can be given regarding the character of Jesus' teachings is that they are still changing the course of men and of nations throughout the world today. Now, as before, those who listen to Him inevitably say, "No man ever spoke like this man!"[10]

Without question, the greatest teaching of Jesus was that salvation comes not by what man does for God, but by what God has already done for man through His Son, Jesus Christ.

Faith, Not Works

A group of people once approached Christ and inquired, "What shall we do, that we might work the works of God?" Jesus replied, "This is the work of God, that you believe on Him whom [God] hath sent."[11]

Salvation by faith — not works — is a supernatural teaching because every man-made religion of the world teaches that man is saved (if there is a concept of salvation in that particular religion) by his good deeds.

Jesus repeatedly emphasized good works, but never as a means to salvation. Further, the Bible teaches that good works are produced in us by the Holy Spirit from the moment we place our faith in Christ and are indwelt by the Spirit.

This truth is revealed clearly in God's Word: "For by grace you have been saved through faith; and that not of yourselves, it is the gift of God."[12]

Another truth that revolutionized the first-century Roman world and continues to change the lives of all who obey Christ's command is His emphasis on love. He commands us to love God with all our heart, soul and mind. "This is the first and greatest commandment. The second most important is similar: 'Love your neighbor as much as you love yourself.' All the other commandments and all the demands of the prophets stem from these two laws and are fulfilled if you obey them. Keep only these and you will find that you are obeying all the others."[13]

Christ also commands us to love our enemies.[14] And He demands that we love each other and thus prove to the world that we are His disciples.[15] Through the inspiration of Christ's

resurrection life, the apostle Paul in I Corinthians 13 wrote a
great definition of love and a further command to love.

No one before or since has so taught and demonstrated by
his life and by his death for our sins the supernatural power of
love.

A Life of Miracles

In addition to His supernatural teachings, Jesus caused
the blind to see, the deaf to hear, the lame to walk and the dead
to live again — all so that men would believe in Him as the
Holy One of God.

Time and again, crowds of people watched in amazement
and said, "He has done all things well."[16]

Jesus is still doing all things well; He is still working
miracles through the lives of His followers today. All that He
wants of us is what He expected when He invited Peter to join
Him in walking on the water: *have faith and never doubt.*[17]

As we have seen, it was prophesied that Jesus would come
into the world to "die for our sins." In the Old Testament, the
Israelites atoned for their sins by offering sacrifices — a lamb,
a dove, or an ox. The sacrifices were brought to the priests, and
the blood of the slain animals was then sprinkled on the altar
as a covering for the sins of the one making the sacrifice.

Now, as explained in Hebrews 10:1-24, such sacrifice is no
longer needed, because Christ sacrificed Himself for the sins
of all men. According to John 1:29, He is the "Lamb of God who
takes away the sin of the world."

Colossians 1:13,14 further explains the supernatural
power of His crucifixion. Paul writes, "For He has rescued us
out of the darkness and gloom of Satan's kingdom and brought
us into the kingdom of His dear Son, who bought our freedom
with His blood and forgave us all our sins."

Unique Significance

The deaths of Socrates, Mohammed, Buddha, Confucius,
or any other man who has ever lived have no significance for
us. But the death of Jesus Christ has resulted in our being
freed from the penalty of sin and death.

The Bible says, "For all have sinned and fall short of the
glory of God."[18] It also makes it clear, "the wages of sin is

death."[19] Christ came to bridge the chasm between a holy God and sinful man by giving Himself as a sacrifice for us.

No one else has ever done that. No one else can do it, for God's Word assures us "there is salvation in no one else, for there is no other name under heaven given among men by which we must be saved."[20]

As a young skeptic, I had difficulty believing in the resurrection, for I could not believe in the supernatural. But as I became aware of the uniqueness of Jesus and of the different quality of life that was His, I was forced to reconsider the biblical claim to His resurrection.

A Matter of Fact

Since it is a matter of historical fact that the tomb in which His dead body was placed was empty three days later, I tried to figure out how the tomb could have been empty on any other basis than the biblical claim that He had been raised from the dead. As I investigated in my studies, I learned that there were three different theories explaining the empty tomb. First, it is possible that He was not really dead and had recovered in the cool of the tomb (this notion is today expounded by certain skeptics under the name "The Swoon Theory"). Second, it is possible that Jesus' body was stolen by His enemies; or third, that it was stolen by the disciples.

During my visits to Jerusalem, I have sat in the tomb where it is believed that the body of our Lord was placed, so I know that a man who had been through the agony of crucifixion and the resultant loss of blood could not have pushed aside that heavy stone — nor could any man for that matter, regardless of how strong.

On the other hand, neither did it make sense to me that Christ's enemies would have stolen the body and then not have produced it when faith in Christ and His resurrection began to spread. You can be sure that they would have produced the body in order to discredit the claim of His resurrection if there had been a body to produce.

The third alternative did not seem possible either. If the disciples had stolen the body, it is unthinkable that they would have been willing to die as martyrs for preaching about the resurrection of Jesus. Yet tradition tells us that all but John did die in this manner — and he died in exile after being

boiled in oil for preaching the good news of the resurrection of
Jesus of Nazareth.

In fact, this is the most convincing argument *for* the resurrection of Jesus to me. The disciples who deserted Jesus at His
trial and crucifixion were the same men who, having seen
Him after His resurrection, spent the rest of their lives telling
everyone who would listen, even at the cost of their lives, that
Jesus is alive.

Only One Alternative

The only logical alternative was that Jesus was actually
and supernaturally raised bodily from the dead as the Bible
tells us He was.

Jesus is the only person who has ever predicted His own
resurrection.[21] He said He would be raised from the dead on
the third day after dying on the cross for our sins, and He was!
Further, He was seen on many different occasions after His
resurrection — once by as many as 500 people. And He still
lives today in the hearts of all who have placed their faith in
Him, demonstrating His life of love and forgiveness through
them.

Whenever men meet Christ, they are changed. The whole
course of history has been changed because of Him. As someone has said, "History is His story."

"The gospel not only converts the individual," someone
has said, "but it changes society." Everywhere the gospel has
been preached it has established standards of hygiene and
purity, promoted industry, elevated womanhood, restrained
anti-social customs, abolished human sacrifices, organized
famine relief, checked tribal wars and changed the social
structure of society.

Phillip Schaff, well-known historian and author, once
said: "Jesus of Nazareth, without money and arms, conquered
more millions than Alexander, Caesar, Mohammed, and
Napoleon; without science and learning He shed more light on
things human and divine than all the philosophers and
scholars combined; without the eloquence of school, He spoke
words of life such as were never spoken before, nor since, and
produced effects which lie beyond the reach of orator or poet.
Without writing a single line, He has set more pens in motion
and furnished themes for more sermons, orations, dis-

cussions, works of art, learned volumes, and sweet songs of praise than the whole army of great men of ancient and modern times. Born in a manger and crucified as a malefactor, He now controls the destinies of the civilized world and rules a spiritual empire which embraces one-third of the inhabitants of the globe."

Blessings and Benefits

Jesus' gifts to all who will accept them are supernatural and include, for example, pardon for sins. He proved His love for us in that while we were still sinners Christ died for us.[22]

As the Prince of Peace, Jesus gives peace of heart and mind: "Peace I leave with you . . . not as the world gives do I give to you. Let not your hearts be troubled, neither let them be afraid."[23]

He gives power to live holy, fruitful lives.[24] He gives purpose, direction and meaning to life: "The steps of good men are directed by the Lord."[25] He gives both an abundant life[26] and eternal life.[27] In addition, He takes away all fear from those who trust in Him: "Perfect love casteth out fear."[28]

Romans 8:34 records that it is Christ Jesus "who died for us and came back to life again for us and is sitting at the place of highest honor next to God, pleading for us there in heaven" (Living).

Again, in Hebrews 7:25, Jesus is described as being of the highest priestly order, that of Melchizedek. In this divine role, He "is able for all time to save those who draw near to God through Him, since He always lives to make intercession for them."

Think of it! Christ's forgiveness is so great and compassionate that He will not allow anything or anyone to condemn us. Even though He is "holy, blameless, unstained, separated from sinners, and exalted above the heavens," He still cleanses us from all unrighteousness and gives us absolute assurance that nothing can ever "separate us from the love of God, which is in Christ Jesus our Lord."[29]

More than anything else, I was drawn to Christ because of His love for me. The Bible says that Christ proved His supernatural love for us by coming "to die for us while we were still sinners."[30]

One day as I was reading the prayer of Jesus to God the Father in John 17:23, I leaped from my chair in excitement when I realized that God loves us as much as He loves His only begotten Son! What is more, He loves us unconditionally. That means He loves us not because we are good enough or worthy of His love but simply because of who He is.

Of course, the miracle of it all is that when Jesus, who is the incarnation of God's love, comes to live within us, that same supernatural love becomes operative within us, enabling us to love others supernaturally as well.

Since there is much more to say on this particular point, Chapter 8, "How to Love Supernaturally," will explore in further detail the great magnitude of God's love for us.

Overwhelming Evidence

Several years ago I had the privilege of meeting with a world-famous theologian. This great scholar denied the deity of Christ and taught the seminarians who studied under him that Jesus was only a great man and a great teacher — but not God incarnate.

As we met together in his office, he asked, "What do you tell a college student when he asks you how to become a Christian?"

Because of his reputation as a skeptic, I questioned his sincerity in asking. But when I became aware that he was genuinely interested in finding the answer to the question, I proceeded to explain why men need Christ as their Savior and how anyone who wants to can receive Him.

Even as I was talking, he interrupted me by saying, "I have rejected Jesus Christ as the Son of God all my life, but recently I have been studying the historical evidence concerning who He is. As I have recognized His influence in history, read the claims of the Scriptures, and considered the lives of His followers, I have become convinced that Jesus is indeed the Son of God."

He then made a profound statement which has been confirmed time and again throughout the many years of my ministry. He said, "I am now persuaded that no honest person who is willing to consider the overwhelming evidence proving the deity of Christ can deny that He is the Son of God."

And this great scholar who had denied the deity of Christ all his life and taught thousands of his seminary students to think likewise bowed in prayer to receive Christ into his life as Savior and Lord.

Jesus Christ stands out clearly as the one supernaturally unique figure in all of history. He is incomparable. He invites all who will to experience His love and forgiveness — "Come unto me." He welcomes "all you who are weary and heavy-laden, and I will give you rest . . . My yoke is easy and My load is light."[31]

One cannot ignore this one who is the central figure of history. Neither can one simply dismiss Him as a great teacher. He claimed to be — and the facts of history confirm that He is — the Son of God. You must either accept Him as such or reject Him. You dare not be indifferent to Him.

Determining Priorities

Some time ago, a famous and eminently successful statesman reacted negatively to my challenge for him to share his Christian faith. "I believe that religion is personal and private, not something to wear on your sleeve," he said. "I am a Christian, but I don't want to talk about it."

I reminded him that Jesus loved him enough to die for him and that the disciples were so convinced of the urgency of passing this message on to others in obedience to our Lord's command that they and millions like them died as martyrs getting the message through to us. Further, I reminded him of the words of Jesus, "He who is not with Me is against Me,"[32] and "Whosoever therefore shall confess Me before men, him will I confess also before My Father which is in heaven. But whosoever shall deny Me before men, him will I also deny before My Father which is in heaven."[33]

He was very sobered by our conversation and after a few minutes interrupted me. "I agree with you. I realize now how wrong I have been. I had never realized how far off course I had gotten. I need to rethink all of my priorities and give Christ His rightful place in my life."

Could it be, dear reader, that you, too, need to rethink your priorities and give Christ His rightful place of authority in your life?

If you have not already done so, why not invite the incomparable Son of God into your life to live His supernatural power in and through you from this moment on?

If you have never taken this step, I invite you to pray the following prayer as an expression of your gratitude for all that God has done for you. Jesus will come into your life as He promised in Revelation 3:20, "Behold, I stand at the door [the door of your heart, your intellect, your emotions, your will] and knock. If you hear My voice and open the door I will come in. . . ."

John 1:12 also assures us that as many as receive Jesus Christ, to them God gives the right and power to become His sons.

You Can Be Certain

If you are not absolutely sure that Christ is in your life, that you would go straight to heaven if you died today, you can be sure in the next few moments. I explained earlier in this chapter that the Bible makes it clear that salvation is a gift of God which we receive by faith — there is no possible way to earn the *gift* of salvation. So, by faith, right now respond to the invitation of Jesus and open the door of your life to Him: "Lord Jesus, I need You. Thank You for dying on the cross for my sins. I open the door of my life and receive You as my Savior and Lord. Thank You for forgiving my sins and giving me eternal life. Take control of the throne of my life. Make me the kind of person You want me to be. Enable me to live a supernatural life beginning today. Amen."

If you asked Christ to come into your life in faith, trusting that He has answered your prayer even as He has promised, then know with absolute certainty that He has done so.[34] What is more, He has also promised never to leave you.[35] So there is no need to ask Him into your life again. Rather, thank Him at the beginning of each day that He lives within you and continue to thank Him for His indwelling presence and power to use you to make His love and forgiveness known to others.

In the following chapters, you can learn more of how to experience the exciting, supernatural life of abundance and adventure that this incomparable one, the Lord Jesus Christ, has promised to all who follow Him in faith and obedience.

CHAPTER THREE

A Call to Supernatural Living

As a young Christian, I was confronted with the words of Jesus: "Anyone believing in Me shall do the same miracles I have done, and even greater ones, because I am going to be with the Father. You can ask Him for *anything,* using My name, and I will do it, for this will bring praise to the Father because of what I, the Son, will do for you. Yes, ask *anything,* using My name, and I will do it!"[1]

I didn't know what to make of that promise because I had never met anyone who ever talked or acted as though he really believed it. I had never met anyone who was willing to believe that God could do miracles, to do the impossible.

I discussed the promise with some of my professors and fellow students in theological seminary. Incredibly, the power and true meaning of those words had somehow never really registered with any of them. And yet, the promise is unmistakable: *anyone* believing in Jesus can ask *anything,* using His name, and He will do it!

Why? Because of who Jesus is. There is tremendous power in the name and person of the Lord Jesus Christ. To Him, God has given all authority in heaven and earth.[2] He is, in fact, "the visible expression of the invisible God. . . . Through Him, and for Him . . . were created power and dominion, ownership and authority."[3]

By promising that we would be able to do "even greater miracles," Jesus is not necessarily referring to His ability to heal the sick and raise the dead. There is a greater power, I believe, and that is for us to be channels of God's truth and grace to help liberate men and women from "the darkness and gloom of Satan's kingdom" and introduce them into the glorious kingdom of God's dear Son, the Lord Jesus Christ, through whom we are forgiven all of our sins.[4]

I believe this power is greater than all others because the sick body that is healed and the dead body that is raised will still die. But the person who is redeemed by the Lord Jesus Christ will inherit eternal life.

Two Kingdoms

According to Scripture, there are two kingdoms in this world: Satan's and that of the Lord Jesus Christ. There are no other kingdoms. Everyone on the face of this earth belongs to one of these two kingdoms — Satan's or Christ's.

God's Word commands us to live in a manner that is uniquely different from those who are a part of the worldly kingdom of Satan. We who are members of Christ's kingdom are commanded and enabled by God to live holy lives.

One cannot read the opening verses of the third chapter of Colossians without recognizing that Christians are called of God to live a quality of life that is distinguishably different from others in the world: "Since you became alive again, so to speak, when Christ arose from the dead, now set your sights on the rich treasures and joys of heaven where He sits beside God in the place of honor and power. Let heaven fill your thoughts; don't spend your time worrying about things down here. You should have as little desire for this world as a dead person does. Your real life is in heaven with Christ and God."[5]

At the same time, God has called us to be "beacon lights," holding out "the Word of Life" to a dark world.[6] Thus, Christians are the ones who should be on the creative, cutting edge in all the sciences and arts. Christians should be the ones interpreting culture according to the Word of God, as so many generations of Christians before us have done.

If we are to face the challenge of our times, I believe it is important for us to begin to live supernatural lives. The Word of God reminds us, "If any man be in Christ, he is a new creature: old things are passed away; behold, all things are become new."[7]

We Are Special

There are many passages in Scripture which assure us that when each of us becomes a child of God he becomes someone special. He is no longer an ordinary person — there is royal blood in his veins.

On thousands of occasions I have witnessed the dramatic and often immediate change which Christ makes when He enters a life. While writing this chapter, I saw this illustrated in the life of a woman whom I met while speaking at a pastors' seminar. I had just returned to my hotel room when the maid walked in. I was immediately impressed by the fact that she was a conscientious and diligent worker.

She told me that she was not a Christian but had often tried to talk to the Lord and often meditated on the things of God. She also told me how her family took her for granted and rarely showed her any kindness, even though she turned over most of her paycheck to them weekly. My heart began to melt as she told me how she wondered whether it was really worth the effort to work so hard only to be unappreciated and unloved.

As we talked, I told her of God's love for her and read to her from the Four Spiritual Laws, which contain the basic truths of the gospel. I asked her if she would like to receive Jesus Christ as her Savior and Lord and begin to experience God's love and wonderful plan for her life.

Without any hesitation, she said that she would, and so we knelt to pray. When we finished, her face immediately began to radiate, and she said, "When you were praying for me, it was as though my mind was opened and suddenly all of the burden was gone. Now my heart is filled with joy."

I went away praising God for allowing me the privilege of helping to lead that dear one, who is as precious to Him as the leader of any country, into the kingdom of our Lord Jesus Christ.

Interestingly, just hours before in that same city, I had counseled a very wealthy and influential businessman who was facing a serious, personal problem. By God's grace, his burden was also lifted as we prayed together, and he, too, received Christ.

As I left on the plane, I was struck with the tremendous contrast I had just witnessed. Here was a man of great influence, worth many millions of dollars . . . and here was a simple woman who made only a few hundred dollars a month, and most of that she gave away — and yet, they were both equal and precious in God's sight.

God had allowed me in the name and power of Jesus Christ to be a part of Him in doing a "greater" work — of helping to liberate others from Satan's kingdom of darkness into His kingdom of light.

Conforming or Reforming?

For some years I have had a growing concern that many Christians of our day are being conformed to the way of the world, to the thinking, attitudes and life-style of secular society, despite the admonition of God's Word expressed in Romans 12: "And so, dear brothers, I plead with you to give your bodies to God. Let them be a living sacrifice, holy — the kind He can accept. When you think of what He has done for you, is this too much to ask? Don't copy the behavior and customs of this world, but be a new and different person with a fresh newness in all you do and think. Then you will learn from your own experience how His ways will really satisfy you."[8]

Another translation reads this way: "Don't let the world around you squeeze you into its own mold."[9] Yet this, I am afraid, is exactly what has happened to most of the Christian world.

Our Lord has commanded us to be the "salt" of the earth and the "light" of the world, but there is really little Christian influence in any facet of our society today. Even though education was born in the heart of the church, today we as Christians have a negligible influence upon the philosophy and emphasis of education, which is becoming increasingly anti-Christian and anti-God.

As mentioned in the introduction, Christians seem to have very little influence in the media, government, business, professions and the arts. The pressures of a godless educational system, the decadence of television and movies and the secularization of our society as a whole have produced a generation which has difficulty distinguishing between right and wrong. Not even the Christian is immune from the world's pervasive influence.

For example, a recent staff applicant saw nothing wrong with having premarital sex with his girlfriend, though both were Christians. When confronted with the scriptural instructions warning against fornication, he admitted that he had never heard this before. On the contrary, he had been told by his professors and contemporaries that sex before marriage was a good way to determine marital compatibility.

In contrasting the life-style of the world with that expected of Christians by the Word of God, there is no more appropriate description of what is happening in the world

today than Paul's assessment of the course of events he observed 2,000 years ago: "But God shows His anger from
heaven against all sinful, evil men who push away the truth
from them. For the truth about God is known to them instinc-
tively; God has put this knowledge in their hearts. Since
earliest times men have seen the earth and sky and all God
made, and have known of His existence and great eternal
power. So they will have no excuse [when they stand before
God at Judgment Day].

"Yes, they knew about Him all right, but they wouldn't
admit it or worship Him or even thank Him for all His daily
care. And after awhile they began to think up silly ideas of
what God was like and what He wanted them to do. The result
was that their foolish minds became dark and confused.
Claiming themselves to be wise without God, they became
utter fools instead. And then, instead of worshiping the glorious, ever-living God, they took wood and stone and made idols
for themselves, carving them to look like mere birds and
animals and snakes and puny men.

Natural Consequences

"So God let them go ahead into every sort of sex sin, and do
whatever they wanted to — yes, vile and sinful things with
each other's bodies. Instead of believing what they knew was
the truth about God, they deliberately chose to believe lies. So
they prayed to the things God made, but wouldn't obey the
blessed God who made these things.

"That is why God let go of them and let them do all these
evil things, so that even their women turned against God's
natural plan for them and indulged in sex sin with each other.
And the men, instead of having a normal sex relationship
with women, burned with lust for each other, men doing
shameful things with other men and, as a result, getting paid
within their own souls with the penalty they so richly de-
served.

"So it was that when they gave God up and would not even
acknowledge Him, God gave them up to doing everything
their evil minds could think of. Their lives became full of
every kind of wickedness and sin, of greed and hate, envy,
murder, fighting, lying, bitterness, and gossip. They were
backbiters, haters of God, insolent, proud braggarts, always

thinking of new ways of sinning and continually being disobedient to their parents. They tried to misunderstand, broke
their promises, and were heartless — without pity. They were
fully aware of God's death penalty for these crimes, yet they
went right ahead and did them anyway, and encouraged
others to do them, too."[10]

This letter was written 2,000 years ago to the church in
Rome, and yet is as up-to-date as tomorrow morning's newspaper. It is an unmistakable description of the life-style of
many of the opinion makers who influence the thinking of the
masses throughout the world.

Warnings for the Church Today

Three of the greatest distortions of biblical truth in the
church of Jesus Christ today that have robbed Christians of
their supernatural resources are what I would call "worldliness," a diluted and distorted brand of Christianity, and legalism.

The spirit of worldliness has so invaded and influenced the
church and the lives of millions of Christians that there is
often little resemblance to the biblical description of the New
Testament life-style. What the Christian life-style should be
is described in I John 2:15-17: "Stop loving this evil world and
all that it offers you, for when you love these things you show
that you do not really love God; for all these worldly things,
these evil desires — the craze for sex, the ambition to buy
everything that appeals to you, and the pride that comes from
wealth and importance — these are not from God. They are
from this evil world itself. And this world is fading away, and
these evil, forbidden things will go with it, but whoever keeps
doing the will of God will live forever."[11]

Actually, being materialistic is not necessarily synony-
mous with being wealthy. Even a person of modest means, by
the world's standards, can succumb to the temptation of being
materialistic. The subtlety of this sin lies in a person's becoming enamored with the things of the world. Whether or not a
person has the means to possess things is not what makes him
materialistic — it is the desiring.

If not controlled, such desiring will eventually separate a
person from the supernatural, abundant life which God has
promised to all who walk in faith and seek first His kingdom.

There are laws of the spiritual realm which are as inviolate as the laws of the physical world, and one of those spiritual laws was given by Jesus Himself in the sixth chapter of Matthew: "You cannot serve two masters: God and money. For you will hate one and love the other, or else the other way around. So My counsel is: Don't worry about things — food, drink, and clothes. For you already have life and a body — and they are far more important than what to eat and wear. . . . Look at the field lilies! They don't worry about [their clothes]. Yet King Solomon in all his glory was not clothed as beautifully as they."[12]

Seeking God First

As a young businessman, I had to wrestle with this problem, for I was strongly attracted to the material things of the world. But when I became a Christian, I could not ignore Christ's command to "seek first the kingdom of God and His righteousness."[13]

Since that commitment, made many years ago, I have sought to be obedient to that command. The Lord has blessed me with the fulfillment of the promise which follows: "Your heavenly Father already knows perfectly well (the things you need), and He will give them to you if you give Him first place in your life and live as He wants you to."[14]

God is trustworthy! And the obedient, faithful Christian soon learns that he, like the psalmist of old, can proclaim: "I have never seen the Lord forsake a man who loves Him; nor have I seen the children of the godly go hungry."[15]

Second, there is the problem of a diluted and distorted "Christianity." Adherents to this interpretation of false Christianity often deny the basic, traditional beliefs of the New Testament. For instance, they often reject the divine inspiration of Scripture, the deity of Christ, the virgin birth, the resurrection, and/or eternal life.

At various times in history, individuals holding such beliefs have had a very negative influence on biblical Christianity. Many of our leading theological seminaries have been plagued by an interpretation of Christianity which has been robbed of its God-intended, supernatural power and resources. As a result, entire denominations have been drawn away from their founding and covenant and New Testament belief.

In my many travels throughout the world, I have frequently met with educators who are on faculties of schools which were once Christian in doctrine and purpose but which have now become diluted and even secular in emphasis.

Some "Christian" schools are more dangerous than schools which are known to be secular and antagonistic to Christian beliefs. Unsuspecting parents may assume that a denominational or independent school that calls itself "Christian" is a "safe" place to send their children. Then they discover that the professors of Bible and religion are often committed to teaching a form of Christianity which is foreign to the New Testament. As a result, many students abandon the true biblical faith.

As one chaplain at a famous so-called Christian university said to me with considerable anger, "I would rather have a witch doctor on this campus than you or Billy Graham." Ironically, the cornerstone at the university where this professor, who denies the deity of Christ, teaches religion has an inscription on it dedicating that institution "to the glory of Jesus Christ."

By failing to insist upon the authority of God's inspired Word, great numbers of seminaries and Christian schools have compromised their commitment to Christ and lost their spiritual vitality. To make matters worse, what few committed Christian educators there are in such universities are often either forced to leave the faculty or find themselves rendered ineffective by being a distinct minority.

To the glory of God I want to say that there *are still* a number of Christian schools and theological seminaries which are faithful to our Lord Jesus Christ, and firmly established on the authority of His inspired Word. Parents and students would do well to investigate prayerfully and carefully the schools which they select.

Legalism – the Enemy

In many ways, the most dangerous of the three heresies is legalism. By definition, legalism is the doctrine of salvation and sanctification by works or strict adherence to a religious code rather than by grace through faith.

The apostle Paul was initially a by-product of such a doctrine. In an autobiographical sketch found in the third chapter of Philippians, Paul describes himself as a "Hebrew of Hebrews." He had "been born into a pure-blooded Jewish home," he had been circumcised according to ritual law when he was eight days old, and he had even become a Pharisee. As a result, he had eventually reached the conclusion that "if anyone ever had reason to hope that he could save himself" it would have been Paul.[16]

Having personally experienced the difference between legalism and grace, Paul was able to proclaim with unwavering assurance: "No one can ever be made right in God's sight by doing what the law commands. For the more we know of God's laws, the clearer it becomes that we aren't obeying them; His laws serve only to make us see that we are sinners.

"But now God has shown us a different way to heaven — not by 'being good enough' (though not new, really, for the Scriptures told about it long ago). Now God says He will accept and acquit us — declare us 'not guilty' — if we trust Jesus Christ to take away our sins. And we all can be saved in the same way, by coming to Christ, no matter who we are or what we have been like. Yes, all have sinned; all fall short of God's glorious ideal; yet now God declares us 'not guilty' of offending Him if we trust in Jesus Christ, who in His kindness freely takes away our sins."[17]

Paul also discovered that Satan tries to intensify the struggle between legalism and grace even after one becomes a Christian. A description of the continuing struggle is recorded in the seventh chapter of Romans: "I don't understand myself at all, for I really want to do what is right, but I can't. I do what I don't want to — what I hate. I know perfectly well that what I am doing is wrong, and my bad conscience proves that I agree with these laws I am breaking. But I can't help myself, because I'm no longer doing it. It is sin inside me that is stronger than I am that makes me do these evil things.

"I know I am rotten through and through so far as my old, sinful nature is concerned. No matter which way I turn I can't make myself do right. I want to but I can't. When I want to do good, I don't; and when I try not to do wrong, I do it anyway. Now if I am doing what I don't want to, it is plain where the trouble is: sin still has me in its evil grasp.

From Frustration to Freedom

"It seems to be a fact of life that when I want to do what is right, I inevitably do what is wrong. I love to do God's will so far as my new nature is concerned; but there is something else deep within me, in my lower nature, that is at war with my mind and makes me a slave to the sin that is still within me."[18]

By contrast, Romans 8 describes the Spirit-controlled Christian — one who is experiencing a supernatural life-style: "So there is now no condemnation awaiting those who belong to Christ Jesus. For the power of the life-giving Spirit — and this power is mine through Christ Jesus — has freed me from the vicious circle of sin and death. We aren't saved from sin's grasp by knowing the commandments of God, because we can't and don't keep them, but God put into effect a different plan to save us. He sent His own Son in a human body like ours — except that ours are sinful — and destroyed sin's control over us by giving Himself as a sacrifice for our sins. *So now we can obey God's laws if we follow after the Holy Spirit and no longer obey the old evil nature within us*"[19] [italics mine].

The reason legalism is so dangerous is that it is so subtle in its appeal. It is attractive even to the most sincere Christians, who are genuinely seeking to please God by determining to be "good enough" and to "earn God's favor" through the good works of their self-effort.

Through the years this has been one of my greatest concerns, especially for those who are involved in Christian ministry throughout the world. How often there has been a tendency to forget that "the just shall live by faith"[20] and that "without faith it is impossible to please God."[21] There is a strong tendency to work hard in the flesh in order to please God.

However, there is scriptural warning against legalism; it is found in the third chapter of Galatians: "For as many as are of the works of the Law are under a curse; for it is written, 'Cursed is every one who does not abide by all things written in the book of the law, to perform them.' Now that no one is justified by the Law before God is evident; for, 'The righteous man shall live by faith.' "[22]

Liberation

The story is told of a tyrannical husband who demanded that his wife conform to very rigid standards of his choosing. She was to do certain things for him as wife, mother and homemaker. In time she came to hate her husband as much as she did his list of rules and regulations. Then, one day he — so far as she was concerned — mercifully died.

Some time later, she fell in love with another man whom she married. She and her new husband lived on a perpetual honeymoon. Willingly, she devoted herself to his happiness and welfare.

One day she ran across one of the sheets of "do's" and "don'ts" her first husband had written for her. To her amazement she found that she was doing all the things her first husband had demanded of her for her second husband, even though her new husband had never once suggested them. She did them out of love.

In the same way, God motivates and empowers us to live supernatural life-styles by His love, not by His demands. As we respond to His love, live by faith and obey His commands, we are protected from falling into the heretical traps which, as we have just seen, are severely weakening the church of Jesus Christ today throughout most of the world.

I believe we are to live such supernatural life-styles in the power of the Holy Spirit that the world will look on in amazement and say of us as they did of the first-century Christians, "How they love one another." They will observe that we are different in a beautiful and attractive sort of way: the way we relate to other people, the way we carry ourselves, the way the qualities and character of the Lord Jesus are demonstrated in us, the radiance of our countenances, the confidence of our bearing, the way we eat, the way we exercise, the way we care for and clothe the body — which houses the Spirit of God. Because man looks on the outward appearance, I believe God wants us to be attractive for Him.

Recently it occurred to me that King David wanted to build a temple in which to worship God. Later, that dream was realized by his son, Solomon. But centuries before, God had already created a temple in which to dwell — and that temple is man.

For years it has been my prayer that my life and the ministry of Campus Crusade would be characterized by the supernatural and the miraculous. My associates and I pray that everyone who visits Arrowhead Springs, our international headquarters, will sense the presence of God and experience His love and transforming power.

It Makes a Difference

Again and again, person after person has shared — without knowing of our prayers — how they have sensed the presence and love of God in transforming power at Arrowhead Springs through the various staff members.

As an example, some time ago a non-Christian producer of a popular secular television series visited Arrowhead Springs. After several days of working with our staff, he came to my office. "I am tremendously impressed with all of you people," he said. "You radiate love and peace, harmony and confidence. You are able to do so much with so little.

"There is a vast difference, for instance, in the people who work in your mass media department and those who are a part of my network. I've been tremendously challenged by your people who are so calm and relaxed and work in a spirit of unity and oneness of purpose. It is obvious to me that your faith makes a difference in your lives."

Some of the plainest people from a human perspective become the most beautiful, radiant, attractive people when they become controlled and empowered by the Spirit of God.

Indeed, the external evidences of the supernatural life begin within. Twice the writer of Proverbs was inspired by God to impress this point in Scripture: "Out of the heart are the issues of life,"[23] and "For as a man thinketh in his heart, so is he."[24]

The third chapter of Colossians describes the substance of the Spirit-controlled life: "Away then with sinful, earthly things; deaden the evil desires lurking within you. Have nothing to do with sexual sin, impurity, lust and shameful desires; don't worship the good things of life, for that is idolatry. God's terrible anger is upon those who do such things. . . . Now is the time to cast off and throw away all these rotten garments of anger, hatred, cursing, and dirty language. . . .

"You are living a brand new kind of life that is continually learning more and more of what is right, and trying constantly to be more and more like Christ who created this new life within you. In this new life one's nationality or race or education or social position is unimportant; such things mean nothing. Whether a person has Christ is what matters, and He is equally available to all.

"Since . . . God has given you this new kind of life . . . you should practice tenderhearted mercy and kindness to others. Don't worry about making a good impression on them. . . . Be gentle and ready to forgive; never hold grudges. Remember, the Lord forgave you, so you must forgive others.

"Most of all, let love guide your life. . . . Let the peace of heart which comes from Christ be always present in your hearts and lives. . . . And always be thankful.

"Remember what Christ taught and let His words enrich your lives and make you wise; teach them to each other and sing them . . . to the Lord with thankful hearts. And whatever you do or say, let it be as a representative of the Lord Jesus, and come with Him into the presence of God the Father to give Him your thanks."[25]

Put simply,

> Only one life
> 'Twill soon be past
> Only what's done
> For Christ will last.

CHAPTER FOUR

The Adventure of Believing God

The Christian life is a supernatural life, an exciting adventure which begins with a life-changing, spiritual birth. For those who walk in faith and obedience, it continues to be a supernatural adventure.

But in order to live a supernatural life, it is important to understand certain basic concepts. We must learn to think supernaturally; we must make supernatural plans; we must pray for supernatural results; and we must expect God to work supernaturally.

Think Supernaturally

We are told in Proverbs, "As [a man] thinketh in his heart, so is he."[1] We become what we think. We have been given the freedom and privilege of determining the quality of our lifestyles by the way we think; and we determine the way we think as an act of the will.

According to Scripture, our minds are linked up with the mind of Christ: "We Christians actually do have within us a portion of the very thoughts and mind of Christ."[2]

Therefore, we should study the Word of God daily and diligently, determining as an act of the will to pattern our lives according to His commands and His example. We begin to experience the reality and the availability of the mind of Christ when we literally saturate our minds with His thoughts and spend much time meditating upon His Word.

The first thing I do when I awaken each morning as an act of the will is to meditate on my Lord and to praise, worship and adore Him. The last thing I do before I go to bed at night is to praise, worship and give thanks to Him. Thus, my first thoughts are automatically of Him when I awaken, because all night long my subconscious mind has been meditating upon Him.

Every morning of every day I acknowledge His lordship. I gladly surrender control of my life to Him. I get on my knees and worship Him and acknowledge my dependence upon Him. Then, by faith I claim His mind and His wisdom for direction for every detail of my life. I trust Him to influence and control my attitudes, my motives, my desires, my thoughts and my actions.

I tell Him that I am a suit of clothes for Him and that He can do anything He wants in and through me. I invite Him to walk around in my body, to guide me any place He wishes. I ask Him to think with my mind, to love with my heart and to speak with my lips. Finally, I invite Him to continue to "seek and save the lost"[3] through me.

I am confident that all I have to do for His presence to so guide me is to ask in faith from an obedient life, for the Scripture promises: "If you want to know what God wants you to do, ask Him, and He will gladly tell you, for He is always ready to give a bountiful supply of wisdom to all who ask Him; He will not resent it. But when you ask Him, be sure that you really expect Him to tell you, for a doubtful mind will be as unsettled as a wave of the sea that is driven and tossed by the wind; and every decision you then make will be uncertain, as you turn first this way, and then that. If you don't ask with faith, don't expect the Lord to give you any solid answer."[4]

New Ways of Thinking

If we are going to live supernatural lives and if we are going to demonstrate to others that they, too, can live such a life, then we must begin to think differently. We must saturate our minds with the attributes of God and the truths of His Word.

Perhaps no better instruction for such action can be found than that given by God as expressed in Paul's letter to the church at Philippi: "Always be full of joy in the Lord; I say it again, rejoice! Let everyone see that you are unselfish and considerate in all you do. Remember that the Lord is coming soon. Don't worry about anything; instead, pray about everything, tell God your needs and don't forget to thank Him for His answers. If you do this you will experience God's peace, which is far more wonderful than the human mind can understand. His peace will keep your thoughts and your hearts quiet and at rest as you trust in Christ Jesus. . . .

"Fix your thoughts on what is true and good and right. . . . Think about all you can praise God for and be glad about.

Keep putting into practice all you learned from me and saw me doing, and the God of peace will be with you."[5]

If we are to live supernatural lives, we must saturate our minds with those thoughts which are pure and holy and right and supernatural. We must think like children of the King if we are going to live like children of the King.

Remember, God reveals His will to those whose thoughts honor Him. "Friendship with God is reserved for those who reverence Him. With them alone He shares the secrets of His promises."[6]

Planning Supernaturally

Never allow yourself to be satisfied with what you can accomplish through your finite, self-centered efforts. Do not even be satisfied with the best that "Madison Avenue" has to offer. If you want to live a supernatural life, you must not only think supernaturally, but you also must learn to plan supernaturally.

I remember when God revealed the vision for EXPLO '72. Our staff began to pray and plan for the time that God would call together a great multitude of men and women who would train for a week to learn how to be more fruitful in their lives and in their spoken witness for Christ. To my knowledge no one had ever planned for such a conference before. Certainly we as a movement had never planned such a massive training effort.

Our goal was 100,000 attendees. While over 80,000 came to Dallas, Tex., for the entire week of training, an estimated 150,000 to 200,000 came for the final day of the meeting.

During the two years of preparation, our faith was often tested. There were countless times when, because of limited funds and the sheer logistics and magnitude of the undertaking, that the entire project could have disintegrated, and all of us would have been embarrassed; worse yet, the cause of Christ could have been hindered.

But God is faithful when we trust and obey Him. Those who were a part of EXPLO '72 know that through supernatural plans, faith in God, obedience and much hard work, God met us in an unprecedented way. Today, thousands of those who attended EXPLO are now serving Christ around the world.

It was during EXPLO '72 that Dr. Joon Gon Kim, director
of the Korean Campus Crusade, invited us to be a part of an
even larger gathering of 300,000 for EXPLO '74 in Seoul,
Korea. Again, no one had ever proposed such a huge, Christian gathering for training. There simply had never been a
training project of that size in history. Certainly, there had
never been an entire week devoted to discipleship and evangelism by such a great number of people.

God, however, had impressed Dr. Kim and had confirmed
in my heart to hold such a meeting. As we prayed, God assured
us that this was indeed His will. We were individually and
collectively reminded that if we ask anything according to His
will, God will hear and answer.[7]

Objections Overcome

Dr. Kim then returned to Korea and called a meeting of his
staff to tell them about the vision God had given for EXPLO
'74. One by one, the staff members began to raise objections,
expressing their opinions that such a meeting could never
happen.

After everyone ran out of objections (interestingly, there
were more than 70 of them), Dr. Kim explained that he believed that God had clearly impressed him that they should
undertake this project. After considerable discussion and
prayer, most of the staff agreed to believe God for the impossible!

What happened? More than the anticipated 300,000 people came from all over South Korea and 78 other countries. In
fact, there were 323,419 people who registered as delegates, of
whom approximately 15,000 were pastors and evangelists.
On the evening of the largest attendance, Korean officials
estimated the crowd to be one and a half million. Night after
night, as many as half a million prayed all night, frequently
in the rain.

I shall never forget the first time I went up on the platform
and looked out over that great host of hundreds of thousands. I
was deeply moved by the size and obvious spirit of that multitude. I had never seen such a sight, and I had never felt such
an awareness of the presence and power of God.

In a single evening officials estimated that more than one
million people registered salvation decisions — fruit of an

incredible movement of God. In one afternoon of witnessing by the more than 300,000 trained delegates, approximately 250,000 expressed their desire to receive Christ. And it all began because God touched the heart of one man, Dr. Joon Gon Kim, who believed God could do anything and made great plans in demonstration of his faith.

God truly met us there in Korea in a life-changing way. None of us will ever be the same. According to a recent official government report, the church of South Korea grew in the four years following EXPLO '74 from three million to more than seven million, and it is still booming. It took almost 100 years for the church of South Korea to grow to three million, and in less than four years it more than doubled! There were, of course, other good reasons for this phenomenal growth, but no person knowledgeable about what actually happened would question that one of the most significant contributions was EXPLO '74.

The Challenges Increase

As our knowledge of God and His faithfulness continued to grow, and as a result of the phenomenal blessings of God on EXPLO '72, EXPLO '74 and other major events, our faith in God as a ministry continued to grow.

In 1968, God impressed upon our hearts a prayer target far greater than anything we had ever heard about or even dreamed of. He wanted us to help take "the most joyful news ever announced" to every person in the United States by the end of 1976 and to the entire world by the end of 1980. The magnitude of the task was so great and the possibility of achieving the goal so remote that we were hesitant at first even to share this impression of God with others.

Since I spend most of my time speaking in meetings and in conferences with Christian and secular leaders across America and on almost every continent each year, I had some idea of the enormity of the task and the improbability of achieving such ambitious objectives. Yet the conviction continued to grow — and with it the impression that we were to share this prayer burden with other Christians and encourage them to become a part of the vision.

Obviously we needed the miraculous intervention of God. We needed the God who parted the Red Sea through which the

Israelites fled from bondage out of Egypt, and the God who multiplied a few loaves and fishes to feed a multitude, to work many miracles if the prayer burden which He had given us was to become a reality.

By 1975, our prayers and plans were crystallized, and we launched Here's Life, America, a movement of 15,000 churches of all denominations in almost 250 major cities and thousands of smaller communities to help share the gospel with every person in America. The results were phenomenal and unprecedented. More than 325,000 people were trained to share their faith in Christ with the rest of America. Through the use of radio, newspaper, television, billboards, bumper stickers, lapel buttons, door hangers and other creative means, the "I found it!" campaign was presented to an estimated 175 million people. It is believed that many millions received Christ as a result of Here's Life, America, and it helped contribute significantly to the fulfillment of the Great Commission in America in 1976.

What Next?

But what about the rest of the world and what we believe to be God's instructions to pray and work to help fulfill the Great Commission throughout the world by the end of 1980? Here's Life, World is a strategy involving churches of all denominations and many different Christian organizations which, working together, will help train a sufficient number of disciples in all nations to help take the gospel through every conceivable means to every person in the world. The goal is to help introduce at least one billion people to Christ during the next 10 years, before the end of 1988.

Our staff members, together with students and laymen whom we have trained, have taken hundreds of thousands of surveys in many countries on every major continent. These surveys suggest that an average of 50% of all non-believers are ready to receive Christ as their Savior and Lord the first time they hear the gospel.

Careful research suggests that in order to help reach the entire world for Christ at least one billion dollars will be needed over and above the present budgets of Christian organizations. As we have shared this plan with many pastors and lay leaders, the response again and again has been, "I have never heard of anything so exciting. . . . I have never heard of such magnificent plans to help reach the world for Christ, and I want to be a part of it. You can count on me."

This strategy calls for mobilizing 1,000 leading Christians throughout the world — leaders in business, in professional life, in religion and in government, both nationally and internationally known; men and women who love Christ and who are deeply committed to helping change the world through helping to fulfill the Great Commission.

One such person is Mr. Wallace Johnson, one of the founders of the Holiday Inns and a leading businessman in the world today. He is over 75 years old. When I laid before him this strategy to help saturate the entire world with the gospel, he said, "I have never heard of anything so exciting and so great in my life." He suggested that we have prayer together and slipped from his executive chair to his knees and began to pray for God's blessing on this great plan.

Mutual Excitement

Although Mr. Johnson had suffered a major heart attack some time earlier and had promised his wife that he would resign his positions on the many boards he had been serving, he asked me if I would share the same challenge with her. She also had not been well physically, but she responded with the same excitement of her husband. They both felt that God wanted them to be a part of this strategy. In fact, Mr. Johnson was so moved by this challenge to help change the world that he agreed to be chairman of the international committee.

We met with a similar response when we shared the plan with Roy Rogers and Dale Evans. Roy and Dale have been our close, personal friends for over 30 years. Though Roy is very busy and prefers to avoid the limelight in such projects, as the plan was laid before them, he said, "I would like to be a part." He accepted the vice-chairmanship of the international committee.

Bunker Hunt, another long-time friend and one of the world's leading businessmen, has agreed to be the chairman of the executive committee. And Edward L. Johnson, chairman and president of Financial Federation, Inc., one of America's largest financial institutions, has accepted the responsibility of vice-chairman of this international campaign.

In addition, many other prominent leaders throughout the world have agreed to serve as a part of this worldwide thrust for our Lord. One businessman said, "All my life I have wanted to do something big for God. This is the biggest thing I have ever heard of, and I want to be a part of it."

He is typical of the kind of men who are accustomed to thinking big in business terms, only now they are translating their ability to think big into the kingdom enterprise and are beginning to trust God to enable them to help change the course of history.

Literally every facet of society, business, labor, government, education, entertainment and the media — all of these will be changed because Christian men and women are beginning to plan strategically for supernatural results. They are uniting in the faith that the omnipotent God — who so loved the world that He gave His only begotten Son to die for our sins[8] and who is not willing that any should perish but that all should come to repentance[9] — will enable them to do all that He has called them to do.

As we share this strategy to help saturate the world with the gospel in obedience to the Great Commission of our Lord, we are confident that it is God's will that everyone will have an opportunity to receive Christ. And so we pray with confidence for at least a billion people to come to Christ — as God is impressing us to do according to Philippians 2:3, "For it is God who is at work in you, both to will and to work for His good pleasure." I have learned that whenever God gives us the will to do something, He always gives us the power and ability to do it.

Praying Supernaturally

Remember this great promise of our Lord: "In solemn truth I tell you, anyone believing in Me shall do the same miracles I have done, and even greater ones, because I am going to be with the Father. You can ask Him for *anything,* using My name, and I will do it, for this will bring praise to the Father because of what I, the Son, will do for you. Yes, ask *anything,* using My name, and I will do it!"[10]

When I was a new Christian, God gave me the faith to pray for the salvation of a young executive. That young man received Christ and has been serving the Lord as a minister for more than 25 years with great blessing. Shortly thereafter, God gave me the faith to pray that my father would become a Christian — and again God honored my prayer. I was so excited that I began to pray for several other people — all of whom also received Christ.

Before long, I was praying for hundreds to receive Christ. Time and again, God honored my prayers of faith, and hundreds responded to the claims of Christ.

Over the last 30 years, my faith has continued to grow. God gave me the faith to pray for thousands, and thousands responded. He gave me the faith to pray for millions to come into the kingdom, and millions have responded through the ministry of our staff and hundreds of thousands of Christians whom we helped to train.

God has now impressed upon me to pray for a billion and more people to be brought into His kingdom in the next 10 years — not through the ministry of Campus Crusade alone, of course, but through the combined efforts of all who love our Lord and who are obedient to His command to go and make disciples of all nations and preach the gospel to all men.[11]

That memorable night when over a million Koreans indicated salvation decisions at EXPLO '74, it was as though God said to me, "You have been praying for hundreds of millions to come into My kingdom; tonight I have shown you how quickly a million can be reached for My glory."

God has not changed. He is the same God whom I met 30 years ago. But I have changed. My faith has grown — and it continues to grow!

Our Lord's words leave little room for timidity and unbelief: "According to your faith be it unto you."[12] In short, our Master is calling us, through faith, to pray supernaturally.

And we all should have such expectations when we work, when we pray and when we witness, because it is the omnipotent God who dwells in the heart of every believer. He is the one who will enable us to do what He has called us to do: "I have been crucified with Christ: and I myself no longer live, but Christ lives in me. And the real life I now have within this body is a result of my trusting the Son of God, who loved me and gave Himself for me."[13]

It is not my life anymore, but His. I have exchanged my life — and if you are a Christian, you have also exchanged yours, whether you are aware of it or not — for the life of Christ.

Satisfied With Second Best?

But we must beware that we do not hinder Him by our unbelief, for we limit His working not only when we doubt or fear but also when we are satisfied with mediocrity. Do not be satisfied to live the way you have lived as a Christian, although you may have had a fruitful ministry, because I can tell you that God has something better for you than you have ever experienced — no matter how fruitful your life has been up to this point. I speak from experience, because this year has been the greatest year of my life, and next year will be greater still.

Why? Because the more I walk with God, the more I realize the truth of His attributes: His love, sovereignty, holiness, wisdom and power. The better I know Him, the more I can trust Him; and the more I can trust Him, the more I love Him; and the more I love Him, the more I want to serve Him.

Seek to know the Lord with all your heart. While you may have no difficulty in worshiping the omnipotent God, you cannot really know the God of the Scriptures unless you study His Word. The one who spoke and the worlds were framed is waiting to reveal Himself to you personally.

The Bible says, "Faith cometh by hearing, and hearing by the Word of God."[14] Faith is not given to those who are either undisciplined or disobedient. Faith is a gift of God[15] which is given to those who trust and obey Him. And it is as we master His Word and obey His commands that our faith continues to grow.

It is my strong conviction that it is impossible to ask God for too much if our hearts and motives are pure and if we pray according to the Word and will of God. Remember, it is a basic spiritual principle that whatever we vividly envision, ardently desire, sincerely believe and enthusiastically act upon will come to pass — assuming, of course, that there is scriptural authority for it. It is this principle that is the foundation of praying supernaturally.

As I have shared previously, there was a time when I could believe God for only a few people to come to Christ; and now, I can believe Him for a billion souls. Also, there was a time when I could believe God for only a few dollars, and now He has given me the faith to pray for one billion dollars to help fulfill the Great Commission and help introduce those one billion people to Christ.

I remember the first time I ever asked God for a specific amount of money. We needed $485 for a particular ministry. Even while I was on my knees, God sent a bank draft for $500 by registered mail from Zurich, Switzerland. A man and his wife who had received Christ in my office, upon returning home, had written to say, "Thank you." At the precise moment I was on my knees, God used them to send $15 more than that which we needed and that for which I was praying.

Later, we needed $10,000, and God impressed us to pray for Him to send it. An hour after we prayed, a new Christian whom I did not know well called to say, "I am a new Christian, and I don't know how God speaks to man, but you have been on my mind all day, so I thought it might be that God was trying to tell me something. I thought I would just call to see if you have a need."

I told him we had just prayed for $10,000. He said, "That's a lot of money, but I'll call you back in an hour." An hour later he called to say he would send a check the next day for $10,000 as a loan without interest. He added, "If God continues to bless me and my business, I will give you the money." A year later, God blessed his faith and obedience, and the loan became a gift.

Miraculous Prayer

Some time later, a million dollars was urgently needed for this ministry. During a board meeting one Saturday afternoon, I was strongly impressed by the Lord to suggest to the members of the board to join me in asking God to provide the needed funds in the spirit of Philippians 2:13, "It is God which worketh in you both to will and to do of His good pleasure."[16]

The Lord who impresses us to pray and work for a particular thing can be trusted to enable us to accomplish what He leads us to do. And so we prayed, asking God to send the money supernaturally, miraculously, so that no one would applaud us, and He would get all the glory.

The following Tuesday afternoon, one of my associates came with great excitement into an important meeting to inquire of me, "Do you know Bud Miller?"

I replied that I did not. "Why?" I asked.

"Well, he would like to give Campus Crusade a gift of $1,100,000."

I called Mr. Miller immediately to thank him for his generosity.

He said, "You don't know me, but I have heard you speak, and I listen to your messages on tape every day. God has used you to greatly influence my life. Recently I sold a part of my business, and God impressed me to send you this special gift."

God had answered our prayers in a supernatural way. There can be no question that the gift had to be God's supernatural provision, for I did not even know Mr. Miller. We had never received such a large gift in the entire history of the ministry.

You will be interested to know that God used our new friend to provide these and additional urgently needed funds at a dramatic time in this ministry's history so that we could proceed with EXPLO '74. Though we were confident that the Lord was leading us in all our plans for EXPLO '74, in the fall of 1973, we were suddenly confronted with a serious financial crisis and were faced with a strong possibility of having to abandon the entire effort.

One Man's Investment . . .

Had Bud Miller ignored the leading of the Holy Spirit to give such a large and generous sum to this project, it is likely that EXPLO '74 would never have occurred. Think of it! An unprecedented gathering of 323,419 delegates from 78 countries received a week of training in discipleship and evangelism. Already we can trace the results of that event to millions of people who have received Christ, and Bud Miller has an investment in every one of them.

On the strength of Bud Miller's experience, plus many experiences of my own, I can tell you that it is always best to obey the leading of the Holy Spirit, whatever He leads you to do, or you will miss a special blessing from God and the opportunity to participate in a spiritual harvest.

There was still another time during EXPLO '74 when we faced a financial crisis. Before EXPLO began, 100,000 people — almost one-third of all the delegates — arrived in Seoul for the mammoth gathering without any money. The people had come from all over Korea from almost every village and hamlet. Many of them were from rural areas and had even sold the rice they had grown to put on their tables to eat in order to cover the expenses of their travel to Seoul. They had come trusting that we would provide food and lodging once they arrived, and we dared not turn them away. We invited them to stay as our guests but that decision cost us over one million dollars. Now, we were faced with a monumental financial crisis. Where would we find another million dollars to help meet this unexpected need?

The Father Knows Best

Again we prayed and asked the same thing of God, that He would provide for our needs supernaturally. I kept expecting the telephone to ring any day and hear someone say, "I just happen to have some extra cash, and I am going to send you a million dollars."

But the call never came. Instead, weeks and months passed, and the Lord showed us that He wanted us to reorganize our ministry. Through such reorganization and the elimination of several good projects, we were able to save the million dollars we needed during the following year.

We adopted the policy of zero base budgeting, which means that we carefully analyze the use of money and manpower in such a way as to eliminate every expenditure which does not contribute to priority needs and maximum harvest as it relates to helping fulfill the Great Commission.

Granted, some of the projects and ministries we eliminated were considered important, but they were evidently not God's priority items. I believe He allowed us to have that experience in order to teach us how to be better stewards of even larger sums that He is going to send us in the future. We had always sought to maximize every dollar for the glory of God — which we feel means discipling and evangelizing the largest possible number of people for every dollar invested.

Now we were able to be even more effective stewards for our Lord. Our overhead runs seven percent, and our fund-raising cost is eight percent, both of which are unusually low in comparison to most organizations.

There are times when God answers our prayers as in the first occasion — miraculously. Then, there are times when He answers by saying, "Work harder, save more, give priority to priorities." Both are definite answers to prayer.

Claiming Supernatural Resources

Remember, as believers in Christ we are called to live supernatural lives; we are no longer ordinary people. Our lives are now joined with the one who spoke and the worlds were framed. We belong to the one to whom God has given all authority in heaven and earth — and He has come to dwell within us in all of His resurrection power. Now we can claim with the apostle Paul: "I can do everything God asks me to do with the help of Christ who gives me the strength and power."[17]

So to live a supernatural life-style we must begin to think supernatural thoughts, make supernatural plans, pray for supernatural results and expect God to work supernaturally.

The Muscle of Faith

Do not be discouraged if your faith is still small. Faith, like a muscle, grows with exercise. At this point in your Christian life, you may be struggling to trust God for the salvation of one person, or for $485, or for something else entirely. So stop a moment and meditate on what faith barrier is facing you right now.

Remind yourself of God's power available to you to accomplish the supernatural so that you will soon be able to trust Him for many people to receive Christ and for larger sums of money to be released for you to use in His service.

If one of your problems is the sin of not trusting God (and not trusting God *is* a sin, for the Bible reminds us that it is impossible to please God without faith[18]), why not take a moment and confess your unbelief to God in this specific area and claim — by faith — His supernatural resources.

I invite you to join with me in a prayer which I frequently pray. I am confident that as you truly trust and obey God, He will bless and enrich your life in supernatural ways as He has mine.

Holy Father in heaven, I claim by faith Your supernatural resources so that I can live a supernatural life. Enable me by Your Holy Spirit to think supernatural thoughts, make supernatural plans, pray for supernatural results and expect You to work supernaturally. I pray this for Your honor, glory, worship and praise in the name of Your risen Son, to whom You have given all authority in heaven and earth. Amen.

CHAPTER FIVE

Carnality: The Threat to Supernatural Living

Are you experiencing tension and conflict with your husband, your wife, your parents, your children, your friends? What happens if you are traveling in heavy traffic and someone cuts in front of you? Do you become angry? Do you find yourself cheating, even just a little, on income tax reports or student exams? Do you find yourself critical of others? Are you prone to pass on gossip? Are you frequently jealous, proud, lustful? Have you become lukewarm in your Christian commitment? Have you lost your first love, the love which you knew for Christ when you first believed?

As we have seen, when we belong to Christ, each one of us becomes someone special. We are transformed into "new beings," in whose lives "old things are passed away and all things are become new."[1] Tragically, however, most Christians are not experiencing their "new life" and thus do not live supernaturally.

According to the Word of God, there are three kinds of people in the world: the "natural man" or non-believer; the "spiritual man," the believer who lives by faith and obeys God through the enabling of the Holy Spirit; and the "carnal man," the immature believer who is a Christian but who is spiritually impotent and fruitless.

Another way of describing these three kinds of people is to explain how we have, through the empowering grace of Jesus Christ, been taken from the realm of the "natural" or "unspiritual" life and transformed into "spiritual" beings.[2]

For instance, one of our first experiences of supernatural living as *new believers* is that we are granted insight into spiritual things. We are allowed "to know the Lord's thoughts" and "to discuss them with Him."[3] In our prayer lives we experience the power He has granted us literally to move the hands of God by prayer.

In I Corinthians 3, however, we are introduced to the third kind of person: the carnal man. This person is a Christian who has experienced the forgiveness of sin, the removal of guilt and the joy and blessing of fellowship with God. But through spiritual ignorance or disobedience, he has lost personal contact with God and does not know how to recapture that lost fellowship.

On the other hand, having experienced a new birth and the joy of his salvation, he can never be satisfied with the "natural" life again. Unfortunately, in his search for happiness and fulfillment, he has lapsed into becoming self-centered instead of Christ-centered.

Remember, It's Supernatural

As a result, the carnal Christian increasingly becomes confused and frustrated and does not know what to do about his condition. He is prone to live by his feelings rather than by faith. He tries to live the Christian life in his own effort rather than trusting in the indwelling Christ, for he does not know how to stop being carnal and to again become spiritual.

We must remember that the Christian life is a supernatural life. The only one who can live the Christian life is Jesus Christ. This means it is not what we do for God that counts but what we allow Jesus Christ to do in and through us. Apart from faith in Christ, we cannot become Christians, and apart from moment by moment faith and dependence on Him, we cannot live the supernatural quality of Christian life to which God has called us and enabled us to live by faith.

From thousands of surveys taken all over the world, approximately 95% of all professing Christians identify themselves as carnal, not because they want to be carnal, but because they do not know how to be spiritual. They simply do not understand how to draw upon the supernatural, resurrection resources of Christ by faith. Consequently, they live in spiritual poverty, not knowing or experiencing their great riches and resources in Christ.

As a new Christian, I was puzzled that sometimes learned professors and other intellectuals were antagonistic to Christ and the Christian faith. How could this be? To me the evidences proving the deity of Christ were so conclusive and convincing and the benefits of following Him so great that I wondered how any intelligent person could say "no" to Him as Savior and Lord.

Spiritual Illiteracy

Then one day I read in I Corinthians 2:14, "But the man who isn't a Christian can't understand and can't accept these thoughts from God which the Holy Spirit teaches us. They sound foolish to him, because only those who have the Holy Spirit within them can understand what the Holy Spirit means." Since this discovery I have observed that there are many people who are learned and scholarly in their own areas of specialty and expertise but are *spiritually* illiterate — they have never taken the time to study the Bible and explore the thoughts and writings of great scholars and stalwarts of the Christian faith through the centuries.

Such people either have not known or have not understood that spiritual insight and understanding come only from the Holy Spirit's presence within an individual's life upon acceptance of Jesus Christ. The moment we become children of God through faith in Christ, we become heirs of God, and all of the resources to live His quality of life are made available to us.

But the same limitations on spiritual power and understanding experienced by one who has never met Christ are also felt by the carnal Christian. For example, our Lord commands us to love God with all our hearts, souls and minds, to love our neighbors as ourselves, and to love our enemies. Only a Spirit-filled Christian is able to fully obey that command. The carnal Christian is not only incapable of loving in this way but also often has little desire to love others, especially his enemies.

Carnality and Conflict

Often, carnal Christians are even more miserable and frustrated than non-believers and frequently do more to hinder the cause of Christ than those who do not know our Lord. There are few churches which have not experienced internal conflicts, such as occur between the minister and other staff members, among board members and even among members within the church.

Paul encountered this same situation in the church at Corinth. There, the apostle had to address himself to Christians who were arguing and quarreling among themselves: "Some of you are saying, 'I am a follower of Paul'; and others say that they are for Apollos or for Peter; and some that they alone are the true followers of Christ. And so, in effect, you have broken Christ into many pieces."[4] I believe that now, as then, such conflicts can be traced to a carnal spirit.

I recall a young businessman who came to me one day greatly distressed and angry. He said, "My church is going to split right down the middle. Half of us are going to move out and start another church."

From his critical attitude it soon became apparent that he was one of the problems. So I began to talk to him about the Spirit-filled life, about trusting God and letting Him be the one to solve the problems. I explained to him how he could be a Spirit-filled man.

Then we got down on our knees to pray. He surrendered his life to Christ and asked God to forgive him. When we stood to our feet, he was a changed person and quickly volunteered, "There won't be any split in my church now." I asked him what he meant, and he replied, "I'm the one who has been causing all the problems."

In one of my messages, I shared this story, and a dedicated young Christian told me that the same situation existed in his city. He said, "My father is a very strong-willed lay leader of the church, and he has been a source of contention within the church for many years. He is a very religious man. But the congregation is split over some differences which my father has with the minister and some other laymen of the church."

A Family Affair

The young man asked if I would counsel with his father. The carnal father did not realize that because of his stubborn self-will he was not only hurting the church, but also he was hurting his own family. Thankfully, the members of his family were spiritually mature enough to know that he was the one at fault and were praying that he would become a Spirit-filled man.

From this and other examples, I think Christian parents who are not allowing Christ to control their lives need to recognize that as professing believers they may be communicating to their own children a contradiction of their commitment to Christ. They may be doing such irreparable harm to their families that their children will literally grow up to hate God and the church and eventually want nothing to do with Christianity.

I mention this because many of these young people today are in prominent positions in government, in the media, and in education, and many of the decisions they make will undoubtedly reflect their rejection of biblical truth. The saddest part of all is they have rejected a *distortion* of biblical truth as expressed through the lives of their parents or members of their church. They simply have not been able — nor have they been helped — to make the distinction between true Christianity and its counterfeit.

True and False

What is the distinction between the true and false expressions of Christianity? True Christianity is that which produces a transformed, supernatural life-style. The apostle John writes, "And how can we be sure that we belong to Him? By looking within ourselves: are we really trying to do what He wants us to do? Someone may say, 'I am a Christian; I am on my way to heaven; I belong to Christ.' But if he does not do what Christ tells him to do, he is a liar."[5]

Probably the greatest opposition a staff member faces today, both on the college campus and in the community, comes from students, laymen and others who have been "turned off" by carnal Christians and as a result have concluded, on the basis of their experiences, that they want nothing more to do with Christianity. They have never been exposed to true, Spirit-directed Christianity, which alone can assure them of a life of joy and fruitfulness.

I am persuaded that there are multitudes of people who consider themselves Christians, who give intellectual assent to the deity of Christ and who accept the historical accuracy of Christianity, but their lives show little evidence that they have truly experienced new birth. The above warning of John is clear: Beware of a professing believer who insists on living a life of disobedience to God, ignoring the wooing of the Holy Spirit to live a holy life.

A critical, negative spirit is another manifestation of carnality, and it can do more to sow discord among others than perhaps anything else. This is especially true among Christians. In Proverbs 11:13 we are told, "A gossip goes around spreading rumors while a trustworthy man tries to quiet them." If the "gossip" is equated here with a non-believer, then the "trustworthy man" should, hopefully, be identified as a Christian. But this is not always the case. The carnal Christian all too often falls into the category of his "natural" counterpart when it comes to being critical.

Rumor's Ruin

As Christians, we should never pass on rumors and criticism. Instead, we should seek to quiet them in order to promote unity and love among believers. We should always believe the best. We are to counsel, love, pray for and encourage others, but criticism and judgment of others can be very dangerous.

Though I encourage positive criticism and suggestions from others with whom I work, I try to avoid negative and critical people as if their weakness were a contagious disease — because the results of their influence are often as devastating.

In fact, in Campus Crusade we feel so strongly about the dangers of a gossiping, critical spirit that we have long had a policy that we are not to criticize others. Any staff member who displays a carnal, critical spirit toward another person or organization does so as an act of resignation.

We adopted this policy because we know that a person with a critical spirit disobeys and dishonors God and harms the cause of Christ as well as the person or organization being criticized. They have become "Achans in the camp," and God's blessing is withdrawn from the movement as well as from those individuals' lives.

The Carnality of Criticism

To be critical in a negative, destructive way is a reflection of carnality and results in a fruitless Christian life. I believe that this is an absolute statement of fact — at least we believe it to be so at Campus Crusade.

While Christians should not attack others with a critical spirit, they should be aware that they will themselves often be the target of criticism. This was predicted by our Lord when He said, "The people of the world will persecute you because you belong to Me, for they don't know God who sent Me."[6]

When Martin Luther began to preach "the just shall live by faith," there was a vicious attack upon him personally and upon his ministry by religious leaders. Two centuries later during the Wesleyan revivals, John Wesley was not even allowed to preach in the Church of England and was often pelted with stones and rotten eggs as a reward for his preaching of the gospel.

And at this very moment, throughout the world, there are thousands of Christians languishing in prisons, persecuted by unbelievers because of their witness for Christ. Others who are serving our Lord faithfully do so at a tremendous price.

No Martyr Complex

We cannot expect the world system to applaud us, nor to applaud the cause of Christ. Therefore, we must avoid a tendency toward a "martyr complex" if we undergo pressure as we relate to the secular world. Satan has a well-orchestrated plan, and Christians must be ready for his attacks.

But Satan is a defeated foe — the cross of Christ and the empty tomb were his undoing. As believers we have God's promise that "all the powers of hell shall not prevail against" us.[7] And our victory over Satan comes by faith and obedience, which are characteristics of the Spirit-controlled person, not the carnal Christian.

Feeling an Inner Conflict?

Remember the inner struggle which troubled Paul, as recorded in Romans 7? "Who will free me from my slavery to this deadly lower nature?" Many with whom I have counseled refer to this passage as their "spiritual biography." Does this passage describe your present conflict? Then listen to the good news of Paul's answer: "Thank God! It has been done by Jesus Christ our Lord. He has set me free."[9]

I do not agree with some who believe that there is no "middle ground" of carnality in the Christian life. They feel that, if someone claims to be a Christian but his life is not consistently evidencing Christ-like characteristics, he simply cannot be a Christian. And that if the person's life is manifesting the fruit of God's Spirit, it is a sign that he is a spiritually reborn person.

I do agree that if one professes to be a Christian but deliberately lives his life independently of God, insisting on getting his own way in rebellion against God and having never shown evidence that the Spirit of God is indwelling his life, there is cause for genuine doubt that he has been reborn spiritually.

But I also feel that if a professing Christian has at one time shown evidence of Christ's life within him but is in a temporary stage of disobedience and experiencing spiritual defeat, he is very likely a Christian who is not allowing Christ to control his life and as a result has become carnal. As I have come to understand the Scriptures and have counseled thousands of defeated, frustrated Christians through the years, I am increasingly persuaded that the mirror of God's Word, held up to each person, will reveal to him the true state of his spiritual life and how he can be transformed.

As one man said to me following my message on the difference between carnal and spiritual men, "No one ever told me before that there was such a thing as a carnal Christian. The minute you described the carnal man, I knew my problem, a problem which has plagued me most of my Christian experience. Now that I know my problem, I am ready for the solution." This man soon began to live a transformed life, a life of living in obedience to the control and leading of the Holy Spirit.

Victory in Battle

I am not suggesting here that one ever reaches the point of perfection or "super-spirituality," in which there are no areas of conflict, confusion or frustration. No matter how long one has walked with the Lord, there are times of *temporary* battle between his old nature and the new. Paul describes this situation in Galatians 5:16,17, "I advise you to obey only the Holy Spirit's instructions. He will tell you where to go and what to do, and then you won't always be doing the wrong things your evil nature wants you to. For we naturally love to do evil things that are just the opposite from the things that the Holy Spirit tells us to do; and the good things we want to do when the Spirit has His way with us are just the opposite of our natural desires. These two forces within us are constantly fighting each other to win control over us, and our wishes are never free from their pressures."

For example, it was said of Martin Luther that before he learned the secret of living by faith, there were periods of great depression and discouragement in his life. On one occasion, his wife came down to greet him at breakfast dressed in black.

He exclaimed, "Why in the world are you dressed in black?" She replied, "Have you not heard? God is dead." Luther got the point.

In my own experience, while Christ is almost always a joyful reality to me, there are times when I am fatigued, or I have assumed more responsibilities than I have the time or ability to handle efficiently; then I experience temporary feelings of frustration.

For example, in the writing of this book, for three years I carried the basic manuscript around the world a couple of times, from country to country, continent to continent, working on planes and trains and in hotel and motel rooms, between meetings and between counseling sessions. Now I am several months behind the scheduled deadline for going to press. This has been only one of several super-priorities in my schedule, and I have had to pray often, "Help me, Lord, help me! There is more to do than I possibly can."

But even as I write, the thought comes to mind that perhaps the Lord has allowed me to come to this point of frustration to help those readers who may have come to false conclusions about Bill Bright. Some may believe that I have reached a point of spiritual maturity where the problems of this life do not touch me. I can say, to the glory and praise of God, that usually my experience is one of walking in the joy, excitement and adventure of the resurrection life. But there are moments when I am faced with pressures and frustration which press in upon me.

However, through the practice of spiritual breathing, which I shall discuss later, these times of uncertainty and frustration are fleeting, lasting only a few moments.

How truly liberating it was to me when I discovered *for myself* that one can never live the Christian life through one's own efforts. As we read in Romans 8:7, "The old sinful nature within us is against God. It never did obey God's laws and it never will." But what a relief and great encouragement it is to learn that we can trust Christ to live His resurrection life in and through us. Christ and Christ alone enables us to live the Christian life, and He does so in direct correspondence to our faith and obedience — not because of our self-effort, no matter how earnest and sincere.

What Is Faith?

Faith is simply another word for trust. What is important to know, however, is that faith — or trust — must have an object. The Christian's object of faith is God and His Word. And His Word tells us that we need not continue to be defeated, fruitless, impotent — in short, carnal — Christians. We can live holy, victorious lives and be fruitful witnesses for Christ. That is what He has called us to be. No Christian need continue to be carnal!

It is therefore essential that we recognize that it is our Lord and Savior, Jesus Christ — the object of our faith — who has both the power and the willingness to deliver us from the defeat and frustration of a carnal life. He expects in return only that we place our faith, however weak it may be at times, in Him.

God is trustworthy; His Word is trustworthy. The better we know God, the more we can trust Him; and the more we trust Him, the more we experience the reality of His love and grace and power and the supernatural life which is our heritage.

If you are having trouble with carnality, I have good news for you. The most exciting, life-changing spiritual concept I know anything about will be introduced in the next chapter — the supernatural power of "spiritual breathing." There you will find a way to overcome those areas of conflict in the Christian life, whatever they may be for you — pride, jealousy, lust, the fatigue of overwork, criticism and a thousand others — not by your own strength, but by the power of the Holy Spirit who dwells within you if you have received Christ and have become a child of God.

Before leaving this chapter, however, may I suggest that you pause right now in your reading to pray, asking God to reveal any presence of a carnal spirit in your life — so that you may confess and turn from it. Then thank Him for having freed you from slavery to the lower nature through the sacrifice of His Son, Jesus Christ. Pray for His supernatural presence to make you a "spiritual" Christian, and expect — in faith — supernatural results.

CHAPTER SIX

The Supernatural Power of Spiritual Breathing

If I had only one message to share with the entire Christian world, it would be how to breathe spiritually. Spiritual breathing is as essential to the joy and fruitfulness of a Christian's life as physical breathing is to the physical life. No message I have ever given has been so mightily used of God as this life-changing truth.

It was in Portland, Ore., many years ago when I was speaking at one of our Lay Institutes for Evangelism, that God gave me the term, "spiritual breathing." Immediately, the response to the concept was electric! Never had I received such enthusiastic and positive reaction to a message.

Shortly thereafter, I gave a message on spiritual breathing at an international conference of the Christian Business Men's Committee in Montreal, Canada. Again, the response was most gratifying. Many came forward to say that my message had "liberated" them from legalism. Others who were ready to give up "trying" to live the Christian life were given the confidence that they could now live the victorious life which had so long eluded them.

Universal Response

In another instance, a student approached me saying, "I am a new Christian, and I have tried hard to live the Christian life; but I have failed so many times that just this morning I told God I would never attend another Christian meeting after today and would cease to call myself a Christian, if he didn't show me how to be more successful in living the Christian life. I believe God has surely answered my prayer through your message."

On one occasion, a pastor came running up to me right after I had just finished giving a message and was rushing to catch a plane. "I want to thank you for your help," he exclaimed. "A few days ago I resigned as pastor of my church because I was thoroughly discouraged and defeated. I had reached a point where I couldn't help my people. I was even planning to leave the ministry and get a secular job. But today you helped me to understand how I can live a Spirit-filled life. I am now excited about what God is going to do in my life and in my church."

I give thanks and praise to God for literally thousands of people in many countries on every continent who have indicated similar benefits and blessings through the sharing of these truths about the Spirit-filled life.

Spiritual breathing is the most exciting discovery about the Spirit-filled life that I have ever made. It simply involves confession of sin (exhaling), and claiming the fullness and control of the Holy Spirit in our lives by faith (inhaling). It is such a simple concept that most Christians stumble over it in their search for much "deeper truths" from God's Word.

Personal Experience

From the very beginning of my new life as a Christian, God placed in my heart a strong desire to live a holy life and to be a fruitful witness for our Lord Jesus Christ. I really worked at this matter of being a Christian. I attended church several times each week at the First Presbyterian Church of Hollywood where I received Christ. I was even elected the president of the young adult group and became the leader of a large witnessing group of more than 100 young people. I also served as a deacon in the church.

I studied and memorized Scripture, lived a disciplined life of prayer and witnessed for Christ regularly — often several times each week. Yet, the harder I tried to live the Christian life the more frustrated I became. True, there were periods of great joy, blessing and some success in my witness for our Lord, but there were many times of discouragement and defeat — primarily because I made many promises to God concerning these activities, promises I was not able to keep. As a result, I often felt guilty and spiritually inadequate.

One day I read the account of Jesus casting demons out of a young man when the disciples failed to do so. When the disciples asked why they had not been able to cast out the demons, Jesus replied, ". . . This kind of demon won't leave unless you have prayed and gone without food."[1]

So I decided to fast and pray, sometimes going for a week at a time without anything but water passing my lips. But I saw no change in my sense of spiritual defeat.

Then I was invited to meetings where I was encouraged to speak in tongues. Hands were laid on me, and different people prayed that I would be "baptized with the Holy Spirit." Still nothing happened.

A friend of mine shared a similar experience in his search for the empowering of the Holy Spirit. "Not only did I not speak in tongues, but I continued in my frustration and confusion about the Holy Spirit. I can honestly say that I submitted myself to this matter as completely as I possibly could; and yet, when I did not speak in tongues, I felt a cloud of guilt come over me, and it plagued me for many years."

One day God graciously opened my mind as I was reading His Word and showed me how simply one can appropriate the fullness and power of the Holy Spirit. He revealed to me the concept of spiritual breathing. And now for more than a quarter of a century I have known the exciting, wonderful and adventuresome joy of walking in the Spirit.

My dear friends, this same joy and assurance can be yours! The same cleansing and forgiveness is available to you simply by confessing your sins.

What does "confessing your sins" involve? First, it means acknowledging the sins in your life, whatever they may be: pride, jealousy, lust, dishonesty, a critical spirit or resentment.

It is possible that your sin may be of a more subtle nature, as was the case of the church in Ephesus, where we read in the second chapter of Revelation that even though the Christians had many very commendable qualities, they had "lost their first love" for the Lord.[2]

On the other hand, you may identify with the sinfulness of the church at Laodicea, of which God said, "I know you well — you are neither hot nor cold: I wish you were one or the other! But since you are merely lukewarm, I will spit you out of my mouth!"[3]

Or, it may be that yours is the sin of unbelief. The Bible says in Hebrews 11:6 that without faith it is impossible to please God. Again, in Romans 14:23 we are told that "whatsoever is not of faith is sin" (KJV).

What to Do About Sin

In Greek, the original language of the New Testament, "confession" means to "agree with" or "to say along with." So when we confess our sins or spiritually exhale, we agree with God that we have not been faithful in obeying Him, that by our attitudes and actions and by our thoughts — both spoken and unspoken — we have sinned by falling short of God's *moral excellence.*

Confession involves at least three things. First, we say to God, "I know that this is wrong, and I agree with You that it is wrong." Second, we say, "I agree with You that the death of the Lord Jesus Christ on the cross has paid the penalty for this sin." And third we say, "I repent." This means we change our mind and attitude about whatever is causing us to sin. This, in turn, results in a change of action.

These steps are basic to the act of confession. It is not enough just to acknowledge casually, "Lord, I have failed You." There needs to be an awareness of each of the three parts of confession and application of them to every sin in our lives.

The Basis of Confession

Jesus of Nazareth came to "seek and to save the lost."[4] He came to give His life a "ransom" for others.[5] He did not come to be the greatest leader, teacher and example of all the centuries — though He was all of these and more. Jesus came to die — for you and me and for the sins of all men.

This divine plan of redemption is further revealed in Hebrews: "He [God] cancels the first system [animal sacrifices] in favor of a far better one. Under this new plan we have been forgiven and made clean by Christ's dying for us once and for all. Under the old agreement the priests stood before the altar day after day offering sacrifices that could never take away our sins. But Christ gave Himself to God for our sins as one sacrifice for all time, and then sat down in the place of highest honor at God's right hand. . . . For by that one offering He made forever perfect in the sight of God all those whom He is making holy. . . . I will never again remember their sins and lawless deeds."[6]

Think of it and rejoice! All the sins that you and I have ever committed or ever shall commit are forgiven — past, present and future — the moment we receive Christ, according to God's Word.

Then you may rightly ask, "If all of my sins past, present and future are forgiven, why do I need to confess my sins? Why do I need to 'exhale'?"

According to God's Word, confession is an act of obedience and an expression or demonstration of faith which makes real in our experience what is already true concerning us from God's point of view. Through the sacrifice of Christ He sees us as righteous and perfect. The rest of our lives on earth are spent maturing and becoming in our experience what we already are in God's sight.

License to Sin?

If our sins are forgiven by the death of Christ and the shedding of His blood, what is to keep a person from abusing God's grace and consciously continuing to sin? God's Word answers that question: "The Ten Commandments were given so that all could see the extent of their failure to obey God's laws. But the more we see our sinfulness, the more we see God's abounding grace forgiving us. Before, sin ruled over all men and brought them to death, but now God's kindness rules instead, giving us right standing with God and resulting in eternal life through Jesus Christ our Lord.

"Well then, shall we keep on sinning so that God can keep on showing us more and more kindness and forgiveness? Of course not! Should we keep on sinning when we don't have to? For sin's power over us was broken when we became Christians and were baptized to become a part of Jesus Christ; through His death the power of your sinful nature was shattered.

"Your old sin-loving nature was buried with Him by baptism when He died, and when God the Father, with glorious power, brought Him back to life again, you were given His wonderful new life to enjoy."[7]

A careful reading of I John 2 helps us realize that we will not want to sin if we really are children of God any more than a butterfly would want to crawl on the ground as it once did as a caterpillar. "Someone may say, 'I am a Christian; I am on my way to heaven; I belong to Christ.' But if he doesn't do what Christ tells him to, he is a liar."[8]

Practice Does Not Make Perfect

"The person who has been born into God's family does not make a practice of sinning, because now God's life is in him; so he can't keep on sinning, for this new life has been born into him and controls him — he has been *born again*."[9]

Scripture promises many things about confession. The 139th Psalm concludes with these words: "Search me, O God, and know my heart; test my thoughts. Point out anything You find in me that makes You sad, and lead me along the path of everlasting life."[10]

For those who refuse to confess their sins, there is tremendous conflict, confusion, frustration and an incredible burden of guilt. This is vividly described in Psalms 32 as King David reflects on the anguish of guilt — and the joy of forgiveness: "What happiness for those whose guilt has been forgiven! What joys when sins are covered over! What relief for those who have confessed their sins and God has cleared their record.

"There was a time when I wouldn't admit what a sinner I was. But my dishonesty made me miserable and filled my days with frustration. All day and all night Your hand was heavy on me. My strength evaporated like water on a sunny day until I finally admitted all my sins to You and stopped trying to hide them. I said to myself, I will confess them to the Lord. And You forgave me! All my guilt is gone."[11]

There are many truths in this short passage which are applicable to our lives. First of all, when we refuse to spiritually exhale by confessing our sins, we are miserable. On the other hand, when we do confess our sins, we experience God's complete forgiveness. He removes our guilt and fills our lives with joy — the kind of joy that we will very much want to share with others. The psalmist also knew this when he wrote, "Create in me a new, clean heart, O God, filled with clean thoughts and right desires. . . . Restore to me again the joy of Your salvation, and make me willing to obey You. Then I will teach Your ways to other sinners, and they — guilty like me — will repent and return to You."[12]

Second, we may ask what King David meant when he said, "Now I say that each believer should confess his sins to God . . . while there is still time to be forgiven. Judgment will not touch him if he does."[13] Just as a loving father disciplines a disobedient child, so God in His love for us disciplines us when we are disobedient, according to Hebrews 12:7. Actually, "child-training" would be a more accurate way of describing what God does for us when we are disobedient.

Unnecessary Suffering?

Many Christians unnecessarily go through all kinds of adversity: financial, emotional, marital and family problems, and even physical illness. More often than not, God is trying to get their attention. But because they refuse to listen to and obey Him, they are disciplined and continue in their misery. Beware, of course, that you do not assume that every time friends or loved ones have difficult experiences that they are being disciplined by God because of their disobedience. It may well be that God is working in their lives as He did in Job's — not because of disobedience but to help them mature and become more fruitful and effective witnesses.

However, when you personally are going through adversity, and problems continue to plague your life, you would do well to look into the mirror of God's Word. Ask the Holy Spirit to show you if there is any unconfessed sin in your life. If there is, be quick to turn to the Lord, confess your sins and receive His forgiveness and cleansing in order to avoid further chastening.

I often find that Christians are frustrated because their church is not growing, their personal ministry is not prospering, or their witness for Christ is fruitless. They do not understand why. With few exceptions, I believe circumstances such as these to be the consequences of unconfessed sin.

Again, I would remind you not to judge others when they are having difficulties. It may be that God is simply maturing them for a greater ministry for Him. God's Word speaks to this very point: "Dear brothers, is your life full of difficulties and temptations? Then be happy, for when the way is rough, your patience has a chance to grow. So let it grow, and don't try to squirm out of your problems. For when your patience is finally in full bloom, then you will be ready for anything, strong in character, full and complete."[14]

A friend of mine had been very successful in business but after he became a Christian everything seemed to go wrong. Problem after problem seemed to plague him. Yet he never seemed to be discouraged or defeated. He assured me that there was no sin in his life unconfessed. So I rejoiced with him that God was preparing him for a very important responsibility in His kingdom, which is exactly what happened. He is now the director of a very fruitful ministry for our Lord. The problems and testing served to help equip him to be a better ambassador for our Lord.

Claim Forgiveness

As I mentioned earlier, if you have not already done so, may I encourage you to pause right now, find a quiet place alone, and ask the Holy Spirit to call to your mind everything that is wrong in your life. Take a sheet of paper and write down what He reveals to you. Then claim I John 1:9, which says, "If we confess our sins, God is faithful and just to forgive us our sins and to cleanse us from all unrighteousness." Thank God that He has forgiven you. Thank Him that He has cleansed you. Then destroy the list of sins which you have written down. Do not allow anyone to see your list. This discipline of confession of your sins is strictly between you and the Lord.

If a feeling of guilt continues to persist, you can know that this is not God who is speaking to you, but the enemy of your soul, who is seeking to deceive you into thinking that God has not forgiven you. Ignore these impressions. Claim the promise of I John 1:9 and be confident on the basis of God's own Word that you have been forgiven. Thank and praise Him that all the sins you have ever committed have been forgiven — past, present and future.

Be assured that confession will make real in your experience what God says He will do in your life because of Christ's death on the cross. Be assured also that in having exhaled your sins, you are ready to appropriate the power and fullness of God's Holy Spirit. This involves the next step in spiritual breathing, inhaling — the subject of the next chapter.

CHAPTER SEVEN

Spiritual Breathing — Part II

There is a second essential part to spiritual breathing: *inhaling*. Inhaling involves appropriating by faith the fullness and power of the Holy Spirit.

Before discussing how we take this step, however, it might be helpful to consider for a moment the person of the Holy Spirit — who alone can fill and empower us so that we can overcome the frustration, impotence and fruitlessness of sinful and guilt-ridden lives.

In some theological circles there is much skepticism and hesitancy to talk about the Holy Spirit. We must not forget, however, that Jesus Himself had much to say about the Holy Spirit.

In John's Gospel, for instance, Jesus explained to the disciples that it was necessary for Him to leave them in order that the Holy Spirit could come to them. "He shall guide you into all truth. . . . He shall praise Me and bring Me great honor by showing you My glory."[1]

During the 40 days following His resurrection, Jesus appeared to the disciples on many occasions and to as many as 500 at a single time. At His last meeting with them before His ascension, Jesus said to His disciples: "John baptized you with water . . . but you shall be baptized with the Holy Spirit in just a few days . . . [and] when the Holy Spirit has come upon you, you will receive power to testify about Me with great effect, to the people in Jerusalem, throughout Judea, in Samaria, and to the ends of the earth, about My death and resurrection."[2]

Dramatic Difference

With these promises before them, the disciples — who in Jesus' darkest hour of crisis during the trial and at the cross had deserted Him — went out in their new-found power to turn the world upside down. In obedience to His command, they went forth to preach the gospel in the power of the Holy Spirit throughout the world.

What was the difference? The difference was the Holy Spirit. And the same Holy Spirit — the third person of the

Trinity — still comes today, possessing all the attributes of Deity, to indwell the heart of every believer, and He will never leave. The very moment a person receives Christ he is born again, he is baptized into the body of Christ, he is filled with the Holy Spirit. There is only "one Lord, one faith, one baptism."[3] But there are many "fillings."

Scriptural proof of this can be seen throughout the example of the life of Peter. He was "filled" with the Holy Spirit, as were the other disciples on the day of Pentecost,[4] he was again "filled" with the Spirit as he witnessed with John before the Sanhedrin,[5] and after his dramatic "release" from prison by an earthquake he is "filled" yet again — together with the other apostles — to go out and preach God's message.[6]

Just as the Holy Spirit transformed the lives of the first-century disciples from spiritually impotent, frustrated, fruitless men into courageous martyrs for Christ, He wants to transform our lives in the same way, if only we will surrender ourselves and by faith be filled with His power.

It is the Holy Spirit who makes the difference between failure and success in the Christian life, between fruitlessness and fruitfulness in our witness. In fact, as Jesus explains, it is the Holy Spirit who "bestows this life from heaven."[7] It is through His filling of our lives with God's love and forgiveness that we are "born again" into the family of God.

The Work of the Spirit

It is also the Holy Spirit who illumines the Word of God so that we are able to understand the things of God. In fact, no matter how brilliant and learned a person may be, unless he is controlled by the Spirit, he will not understand what God's Word means. This is the explanation for the many theologians who doubt the inspiration and authority of the Bible. Oftentimes an untrained person, like the original disciples, who is filled with the Holy Spirit and walks in faith and obedience, has a better understanding of the Scriptures than the most brilliant theologians who are not Spirit-filled.

Further, it is the Holy Spirit who enables the believer to live a holy life. If the Spirit does not control us, we cannot bear the Spirit's fruit of love, joy, peace, long-suffering, gentleness, goodness, faith, meekness and temperance.[8]

And it is the Holy Spirit who not only enables us to pray but who also prays on our behalf. Paul writes, "For we know not what we should pray for as we ought: but the Spirit itself maketh intercession for us with groanings which cannot be uttered."[9] Indeed, everything about the Christian life involves God the Holy Spirit.

Often, as I am counseling with believers, I ask them if they are *filled* with the Holy Spirit. The reason I ask is that even though the Holy Spirit indwells each believer, not all Christians are filled and controlled by the Spirit.

Many Christians, when I ask if they are Spirit-filled, assure me that they are, but they do not fully understand what they are saying. Then I explain to them that the Spirit-filled person is one who, according to Acts 1:8, is a fruitful, effective witness for Christ. And the Spirit-filled Christian makes music in his heart to the Lord, gives thanks for everything to our God and Father in the name of the Lord Jesus Christ, and is willing to submit himself to other people, including husband or wife, parents and children.[10] When they recognize that being filled with the Spirit involves much more than they had realized, they are often quick to confess that they are not Spirit-filled at all, but would like to be.

"Inhaling"

After explaining to such an individual the Holy Spirit's ministry and the function of exhaling in the spiritual breathing process, I then share with him the aspect of *inhaling,* as the means of appropriating the fullness of God's Spirit.

What does it mean to "inhale"? Ephesians 5:18 gives us the answer, "And do not get drunk with wine, for that is dissipation, but be filled with the Spirit." The command in this verse is, "Be filled with the Spirit." In the original language in which the New Testament was written, the proper understanding is, "You are to be filled with the Holy Spirit on a continuing basis as a way of life."

Or, put another way, "From the time you awaken in the morning until you go to bed at night be continually and constantly controlled and empowered by the Holy Spirit."

This is not just a suggestion, but a *command* of God for all believers. And whenever God commands us to do something, He always promises to give us the power to do what He calls us to do. The apostle John writes, "And this is the confidence which we have before Him, that, if we ask anything according to His will, He hears us. And if we know that He hears us in whatever we ask, we know that we have the requests which we have asked from Him."[11]

A Matter of God's Will

Now, I ask you, is it God's will that you be filled with the Spirit as a way of life? Of course it is. It is not only His will, but it also is His command. Not to be Spirit-filled, controlled and empowered by the Holy Spirit, is to disobey God and to grieve and to quench the Holy Spirit.

How does one enter into this tremendous, wonderful, adventuresome life in the Spirit? Obviously, by faith. As I mentioned, faith is another word for trust. On the authority of God's *command* and God's *promise* you can now say to the Lord Jesus Christ, "I know it is Your will that I be a Spirit-filled Christian, and You promised that if I ask anything according to Your will You will hear and answer me. So by faith I claim Your fullness."

It is so important to understand the concept of spiritual breathing, because there is not just one "filling" of the Spirit in the Christian life, but many. Because of the continual spiritual battle between our old and new natures, we will have consistent opportunities throughout our Christian lives to appropriate God's power and breathe spiritually.

I had the false idea as a young Christian that if I could just push the right spiritual button, I would be catapulted onto a higher spiritual plane and live there the rest of my life. There are those who claim that if a person has some kind of ecstatic experience, such as speaking in tongues or having a vision from God, he will be changed forever and have no more conflicts, no more problems.

A Winning Battle

That is simply not true. As we have observed, God's Word explains that there is a constant warfare between the flesh and the Spirit. But God's Word also tells us what to do about the conflict: "I advise you to obey only the Holy Spirit's instructions. He will tell you where to go and what to do, and then you won't always be doing the wrong things your evil nature wants you to. For we naturally love to do evil things that are just the opposite from the things the Holy Spirit tells us to do; and the good things we want to do when the Spirit has His way with us are . . . constantly fighting each other to win control over us, and our wishes are never free from their pressures. When you are guided by the Holy Spirit, you need no longer force yourself to obey Jewish laws."[12]

In other words, we cannot live the Christian life through self-effort. We can experience the victorious Christian life only through the enabling of the Holy Spirit.

This enabling power is ours for the claiming, as we have already seen in Romans 8. When I came to understand this, I finally realized that no matter how long I fasted, how much I prayed, how many tears I shed, how many hands were laid on me, how many ecstatic experiences I might have, I could not live the Christian life in the energy of my old nature — the flesh. The warfare will always continue. It goes on in the life of every believer.

Since making this discovery of spiritual breathing, I have walked with our Lord for almost 30 exciting years. I love Him with all my heart, and the one great desire of my life is to please Him and to bring honor, glory and praise to His name.

But the conflict still goes on in my life, as it does in the life of every believer. There are no individuals who will ever reach the point in this life where they can say, "I have no more conflict."

However, to the glory and praise of God I can say that it is not necessary to live a defeated life. The experience of Romans 7 is past for those who discover the reality of Romans 8 — the reality of living in the joy of the resurrection and the power of the Holy Spirit.

Heart Preparation

In order to be filled with the Spirit, there are certain things that must take place in the way of "heart preparation." First of all, do you desire to be a Spirit-filled person? Jesus said, "Blessed are they which do hunger and thirst after righteousness; for they shall be filled."[13] If you do not desire to be a Spirit-filled person, obviously God will not hear a mechanical prayer asking Him to fill you.

Second, the Word of God commands us to surrender the control of our lives to Christ. "And so, dear brothers, I plead with you to give your bodies to God. Let them be a living sacrifice, holy — the kind He can accept. When you think of what He has done for you, is this too much to ask? Don't copy the behavior and customs of this world, but be a new and different person with a fresh newness in all you do and think. Then you will learn from your own experiences how His ways will really satisfy you."[14]

Obviously, one cannot be a Spirit-filled person unless every area of his life is totally surrendered to the Lord Jesus Christ. For some, this kind of commitment is not easy to make. Their views of God are distorted and their own self-images are marred.

The only ones who can know that full and abundant life are those who walk in faith and obedience to our Lord Jesus Christ. Sometimes, however, Christians are misled into believing that when they surrender control of their lives and are filled with the Spirit they will become special targets of Satan and live the rest of their lives in tremendous conflict and frustration. It is the disobedient believer who has not surrendered himself to the lordship of Christ and the control of the Holy Spirit who will experience great conflict and defeat at the hands of Satan, according to Ephesians chapter 6. However, the truly happy, fulfilled Christians are those who walk moment by moment in the fullness and control of the Holy Spirit.

Self-Imposed Problems?

Pause for a moment and consider most of the problems you face today. How many of them are self-imposed, the result of ego, pride, lust, jealousy or criticism? Remember, the Bible says that a person will reap what he sows. So if you are reaping problems which are related to these or any other kinds of negative attitudes, it is possible that you as a carnal Christian have sown the seed in the first place.

I was recently talking with a Christian who was experiencing great adversity, heartache and sorrow. He explained his situation this way: "I am simply reaping what I have sown for years. Had I obeyed the Lord I would have been spared my present heartache."

The Spirit-filled person, however, is one who walks in the joy of resurrection power under the control of the Holy Spirit. He is enabled, through the Holy Spirit's presence and power within him, to live a holy life, one that is pleasing to God. He confidently claims the scriptural promise that God will fight for those who are obedient to Him.

I submit to you that the obedient, Spirit-filled believer is one whose life is lived in a different dimension and on a higher plane than that which the non-believer or the disobedient believer can possibly achieve. In short, he lives *supernaturally.*

A Clean Vessel

Then, after deciding that you desire to be Spirit-filled and after you surrender control of your life, the third step is to confess all known sin, or spiritually "exhale." Obviously God does not fill an unclean vessel. He is waiting for you to say, "Lord, I am guilty of living my own life, doing my own thing, and as a result, I have sinned against You." You may want to list the things that you have done that have dishonored the Lord as He calls them to your mind, if you have not already done so.

Perhaps you are thinking, "Lord, I desire to be filled with the Holy Spirit. I desire to be a man or woman of God. I surrender every area of my life to the control of the Lord Jesus Christ. I turn from all known sins and now by faith I appropriate the fullness of Your Holy Spirit."

If this reflects your heart attitude, remember that you are already indwelt by the Holy Spirit. You do not need to invite Him to come and indwell you. He is already there. You are simply acknowledging His indwelling presence and by faith you are inviting Him to fill you, to control you, to empower you, so that every day He will be the one to direct your steps, guide and empower your life.

Let me make this emphatically clear. You are not filled with the Holy Spirit because you desire to be. You are not filled with the Holy Spirit because you surrendered the control of your life to Christ. You are not even filled with the Holy Spirit because you turn from all known sin. You are filled with the Holy Spirit by faith, and by faith alone — not because you "feel filled," or because you have had some kind of dramatic, ecstatic experience, but by faith — based upon the faithfulness and trustworthiness of God and His *command* and His *promise,* as I have already explained.

If you desire to be a Spirit-filled person, may I suggest that you pray the following prayer:

"Dear Father, I need You. I acknowledge that I have been in control of my life; and that, as a result, I have sinned against You. I thank You that You have forgiven my sins through Christ's death on the cross for me. I now invite Christ to again take control of my life. Fill me with the Holy Spirit as You *commanded* me to be filled, and as You *promised* in Your Word that You would do if I asked in faith. I pray this in the name of Jesus. As an expression of my faith, I now thank You for taking control of my life and for filling me with the Holy Spirit."

The next chapter will explain how you can continue to live a Spirit-filled life through the process of spiritual breathing.

CHAPTER EIGHT

Spiritual Breathing — Part III

Did you pray the suggested prayer found in Chapter 7? If you did and were sincere, you are now filled with the Holy Spirit.

Now, do you know for certain that you are filled with the Spirit? On what authority do you know? You might say, "I feel disappointed — I haven't had any emotional experience." Remember, emotions come and emotions go, and the very act of seeking an emotional experience can be very frustrating indeed.

To seek such an experience grieves the Holy Spirit because the Bible says that the "just are to live by faith"[1] and "whatever is not from faith is sin."[2] If you insist on seeking an emotional experience, whether it be speaking in tongues or some other dramatic evidence of God's anointing you, you in essence are saying to God, "I cannot trust Your Word. I need something more. I must have some kind of emotional experience."

Often, I counsel with those who are looking for an experience. But no matter how hard they try they do not succeed. So they feel like "second-class Christians" and become guilt-ridden and more confused. They assume that God does not love them, and they may soon abandon the Christian life altogether.

Many times, those who have such dramatic experiences later become disenchanted. They lose the emotional experience, and because their walk with the Holy Spirit is not based on the authority of God's Word but rather upon feelings, they lose that joyful experience and spend a lifetime trying to recapture it.

The Feelings Trap

Do not fall into the feelings trap that has robbed millions of Christians who have sought an emotional experience of their legitimate joy and assurance. We are to live by faith and by faith alone. The object of our faith is God Himself, and His holy, inspired Word. There are some 30,000 promises in

Scripture which God wants us to claim in order to live bold, Spirit-filled, joyful and fruitful lives. And those promises are available to you by faith.

But, I hasten to explain, there is nothing wrong with emotions — emotions are valid if they are the by-product of faith and obedience. So, don't be *afraid* of emotions. Just don't seek them. Emotions will take care of themselves as long as we trust and obey God.

As I travel the world, I meet with believers wherever I go who have learned the concept of spiritual breathing. Frequently, I ask, "What is the most important spiritual lesson that you have learned since becoming a Christian?" Most of them say, "Spiritual breathing." This is certainly true in my life.

Of course, the filling of the Spirit is not a once-and-for-all commitment. It is a moment-by-moment walk of faith — a total surrender in absolute obedience.

But in making total surrender to Christ, we have God's own promise that He will protect us from temptation and sin if only we trust and obey Him. As Paul declares in I Corinthians 10:13, "No temptation has overtaken you but such as is common to man; and God is faithful, who will not allow you to be tempted beyond what you are able but with the temptation will provide the way of escape also, that you may be able to endure it."

Thus, when I have not claimed God's promised strength to resist temptation — and I must be honest and say that there have been times when I have failed and have become critical, impatient and unbelieving — I know exactly what to do. I breathe spiritually, exhaling my sin and inhaling God's forgiveness and the fullness of the Holy Spirit by faith.

Walking in the Spirit

Inhaling and exhaling is an ongoing process which alone can enable us to experience the moment-by-moment walk of faith which God earnestly desires to share with all of His children.

I would encourage you to spend time every day studying the Word of God. Paul writes in Colossians 3:16, "Let the word of Christ richly dwell within you. . . ." Remember the parallel of this passage in relation to the passage in Ephesians 5:18-

20, and you will observe that hiding the Word of God in your heart is very closely related to letting the Holy Spirit control your life.

In fact, it is impossible for one who is not regularly feasting on the Word of God and living an obedient, witnessing life, to be a Spirit-filled person for long. Also, no one can be a Spirit-filled person for long who does not regularly share his faith in Christ with others, because it is a command of God to witness. The individual Christian who is not witnessing is disobedient, just as the Christian who is lustful, or proud, or immoral, or dishonest, grieves the Spirit.

So hide the Word of God in your heart, talk to the Lord about everything you do. Make it your practice to discuss with Him your every problem, cast all of your cares on Him, tell everyone who will listen about Him and continue to breathe spiritually.

Obviously, as I have already explained, you do not exhale and inhale as often as you breathe physically. A day or a week or a month or several months may pass before you will find it necessary to exhale at all. As you continue to walk in the light as God is in the light, the Holy Spirit will show you your sin. If you do anything that grieves or quenches the Holy Spirit, He will tell you. And the minute He does, you must confess it, turn from it, and by faith exhale and inhale by appropriating the fullness of the Holy Spirit and keep on walking in the light.

"Search Me, O God"

There are some people who are not willing to forgive themselves when they sin, and they keep on begging God to forgive them. He promises that He will forgive us when we *confess*. He does not say that He will forgive us because we fast and pray and beg and plead with Him for His forgiveness, as I used to do. He says that He will forgive us if we confess our sins, which is an expression of faith. So accept His Word and thank Him for forgiving your sins as He promised.

But don't become legalistic about the matter of spiritual breathing. Rather, daily examine yourself. This has been my prayer for many years, "Lord Jesus, is there anything in my life that is displeasing to You? Examine my thoughts, my attitudes, my actions, my motives and my desires. Is there anything that has caused You to be sad and unhappy with me? If so, I want to turn from it quickly because I want my life to be full of the joy and the power of the Holy Spirit to better serve You. I want my life to be maximized for Your glory. I don't want anything to cast a shadow over our relationship as I walk in the light as You are in the light. I want You to have complete, unhindered control of my life."

It Becomes Second Nature

At first, the concept of spiritual breathing may seem a bit mechanical. I liken it to driving a car. At first you feel a bit frustrated, and you are conscious of every move that you make with your feet, with your hands. This was especially true before the days of the automatic shift. However, after a while every movement becomes automatic. You move your foot at the right time, you shift at the right time, you apply the brakes, and you move along smoothly with the traffic.

So it is as you walk in the Spirit. You find yourself, without any conscious effort, exhaling and inhaling. You even forget the whole concept of spiritual breathing because it becomes so automatic.

You will find that you will begin every day with music and melody in your heart to the Lord as you walk in the fullness of the Spirit. Your days will be full of a vital, personal relationship with Christ. You will be talking about the Lord, and you will be following the admonitions of Scripture. In the process, the supernatural power of God will be released into and through your life, and you will become a part of a world-changing movement — a movement of men and women who have discovered that they can believe God for the impossible.

CHAPTER NINE

How to Love Supernaturally

Several years ago a prominent attorney approached me at one of our Arrowhead Springs Executive Seminars. He had a problem.

He had recently become a Christian, and God was making several meaningful changes in his life. Among other things he had learned as a new believer that he should love others, including his enemies.

But he was experiencing tremendous difficulty loving and accepting one of his associates. In fact, he said, they had literally hated each other for a long time, avoiding each other as much as possible, even though they were both senior partners in a very large law firm. As a Christian he now knew that his attitude toward his associate was wrong.

"What shall I do?" he asked.

I shared with him one of the most exciting and revolutionary concepts that God has ever given to me, a concept from Scripture that has transformed many of my relationships with individuals whom I had found difficult to accept and love. It has been one of the most life-changing truths that I have ever shared with others.

I reminded him of Christ's command for us to love God with all our heart, soul, mind and strength; to love our neighbors as we love ourselves; and to love our enemies.

"Your responsibility, even as a new Christian, is to *love* your business associate," I said.

"Well," he replied, "I could never do that. I don't have the ability to love him. I would be a hypocrite to say I love him when I don't."

I explained to him that this kind of love is not necessarily based on emotions, but is demonstrated as an act of the will, which we must claim by faith. I added that feelings often follow, but we must not wait for positive emotions toward another person in order to begin actively loving him according to the command of God.

I suggested that he go to his partner, explain that he had become a Christian, that God had changed his life and had helped him to realize that his attitude concerning their relationship was wrong. He should ask forgiveness and tell him that he loved him.

My friend responded warmly to my suggestion, "I'm not sure I can do it," he said, "but I'm going to try."

Step of Faith

A short time later, he returned with great excitement and enthusiasm. He reported that he had gone into his partner's office and shared how God had changed his life and his attitude toward him and toward their relationship. When he asked his associate to forgive him for the years of hatred, the man was so overwhelmed that, after a brief conversation, my friend was able to lead his law partner to Christ.

Later, both men came to see me. They were joyful men who had experienced a miracle of God in their lives and in their relationship. I rejoiced as I observed these two outstanding attorneys, who had allowed petty personal animosities to destroy their friendship, discover that the Lord Jesus Christ could enable them to truly love one another.

In more than 30 years of counseling thousands of people about interpersonal conflicts, I do not know of a single problem that could not have been resolved if the individuals concerned had been willing to love one another as an act of the will by faith. Such a statement may sound simplistic and exaggerated. Yet I make it after carefully reviewing in my mind all kinds of conflicts between husbands and wives, parents and children, neighbors and friends, associates in business, and any number of other possible relationships. The love of which I speak is known in Scripture as *agape*.

Agape (uh GOP ay) is one of the four Greek words for "love." In particular, it means "sacrificial, supernatural and unconditional love." It was *agape* with which "God so loved the world that He gave His only begotten Son, that whosoever believeth in Him should not perish, but have everlasting life."[1] And it is *agape* with which we are to follow our Lord's command, "love one another."[2]

"Sacrificial" Love

Agape is best described in the well-known and oft-quoted 13th chapter of I Corinthians:

"Love is very patient and kind, never jealous or envious, never boastful or proud, never haughty or selfish or rude. Love does not demand its own way. It is not irritable or touchy. It does not hold grudges and will hardly even notice when others do it wrong. It is never glad about injustice, but rejoices whenever truth wins out. If you love someone you will be loyal to him no matter what the cost. You will always believe in him, always expect the best of him, and always stand your ground in defending him."[3]

The Bible tells us, "We love Him, because He first loved us."[4] Translators render this passage simply, "We *love* because He first loved us." Either way, it is clear that we as human beings have within us the capacity to love *because God has placed it there!*

He loves us unconditionally, not because we deserve or have earned His love. He loves us in spite of our rebellion toward Him. He loves us because of who He is — because of His own loving nature. In Romans, we are reminded, "God shows His love for us in that while we were yet sinners Christ died for us."[5]

Again and again I have been deeply moved as I have meditated on God's love for me. In His prayer to the Father recorded in John 17, Jesus makes an amazing statement which has had a profound impact on me. He tells us that God the Father loves us as much as He loves the Lord Jesus.[6]

Imagine! God loves you and me as much as He loves His only begotten Son. And the kind of love with which He loves us is nothing less than *agape* — undeserved yet unreserved.

Kalevi Lehtinen, our European director of affairs, experienced the agony of shattering disappointment in his relationship with several other Christians. "In time, I came to a point where I said to God, 'God, I am ready to forgive them if they will just come to me and ask my forgiveness,' " he relates. "But they never came. Consequently, I found myself justifying my bitterness all over again.

"Finally, God revealed to me that forgiveness, like love, must be totally unconditional. I saw that conditional forgiveness is not really forgiveness at all! My forgiveness must never be based upon the other person's coming to me and asking to be forgiven. I must be able to forgive without being asked.

"When I confessed my unloving attitude, God simply wiped all the bitterness away. For the first time, I could forgive unconditionally. Some of the people in question have still not come to me to ask my forgiveness. It is, I believe, a matter between God and them if they come; but, if they do, I will be able to say to them in all honesty, 'I forgave you for that a long time ago.' "

Loving by Faith

As we grow in the Spirit by getting to know God and by learning what He says in His Word, we discover the secrets of Christian living. In making these discoveries, the most important thing we learn is that we cannot make ourselves like Christ *through self-effort*. Change in our lives comes only through the power of His Holy Spirit residing in us, making us like Christ as we walk moment by moment in faith and in obedience.

In arriving at the point in our spiritual lives where we can love supernaturally — or, if you will, become *agape* persons — we experience what it means to become acquainted intimately with the Lord of the universe. We encounter not only the loving attractiveness of His character but also His authority and power.

We learn that He knows all things and yet loves us as no one else has ever loved us. We see His justice, His integrity, His strength, His kindness and His generosity. And we find that seeing Him as He is only causes our love and respect for Him to deepen and grow.

An *agape* person — one who loves supernaturally with God's supernatural love — is therefore one who is committed to growing in the Spirit. Such a person is a Christian who comprehends, embraces and gives evidence of Jesus' divine characteristics in operation in his life. Again, these characteristics are not the result of self-effort. They can become an authentic part of a Christian's life only when he willingly yields the throne of his life to the living Christ and trusts, by faith, to have God's Holy Spirit reside in every facet of his own personal character.

A Personal Crisis

God taught me how to love supernaturally with His supernatural, unconditional *agape* kind of love many years ago when I was faced with a personal crisis. I was having difficulty loving certain individuals whom I felt had been unfaithful to my trust.

God often speaks to me in the quiet of the early morning when there are no telephones, appointments and other distractions. So at two o'clock one morning, at a time when the crisis was mounting, God awakened me from a deep sleep. I took my Bible and knelt before the Lord to read and pray. "Lord," I asked, "is there something You want to say to me?"

For the next two hours God filled my heart with indescribable joy and His supernatural love. During those hours He taught me how to love by faith.

Let me explain. With every command of God there is a promise, either explicit or implied. God commands us to love. We are commanded to love God with all of our hearts, souls and minds, and our neighbors as ourselves. We are also commanded to love our enemies.[7]

There they are, *commands* that are totally impossible for man to fulfill, but not impossible for God. That night He reminded me of His *promise* recorded in I John 5:14,15, that if we ask according to His will He will hear and answer us. Immediately I related God's command to His promise, and a miracle took place.

That night I began to love by faith, on the basis of God's command and promise, those whom I had tried to love unsuccessfully through self-effort in the past. But now, something wonderful had happened to me — by God's grace I was able to truly love them on the basis of God's unconditional love which transcended all the attitudes and actions involved in our relationship.

An Act of the Will

You will observe that the I Corinthians 13 kind of love is an expression of the will. *I chose to love those individuals as an act of the will,* by faith, and the results were miraculous and supernatural. I found that my attitudes and actions toward them were immediately and dramatically changed. Since that marvelous night I have truly loved those whom I had been

unable to love before. And so it has been that through the
years, when difficulties and misunderstandings have arisen,
loving by faith has become an exciting reality in my life.

Indeed, the command to love which had caused me such
anguish and concern previously now became an exciting challenge. I am no longer intimidated and defeated by our Lord's
commands to love one another: "I am giving a new commandment to you now — love each other as much as I love you. Your
strong love for each other will prove to the world that you are
My disciples";[8] "I demand that you love each other as much as
I love you."[9]

Paul also warns in I Corinthians 13 that everything I do is
of no value at all apart from love: "If I had the gift of being able
to speak in other languages without learning them, and could
speak in every language there is in all of heaven and earth,
but didn't love others, I would only be making noise. If I had
the gift of prophecy and knew all about what is going to
happen in the future, knew everything about *everything,* but
didn't love others, what good would it do? Even if I had the gift
of faith so that I could speak to a mountain and make it move, I
would still be worth nothing at all without love. If I gave
everything I have to poor people, and if I were burned alive for
preaching the Gospel but didn't love others, it would be of no
value whatever."[10]

I now realize that everything I do for God must be done in
love or it will be of no value whatever — so I ask God, and
claim by faith His promise, that whatever else He may wish
my life to be, it will be characterized by love, His supernatural, unconditional love.

Now, when I find myself falling short of this standard, and
I sometimes do, I pause and ask God to forgive me and once
again claim by faith His *agape* for those whom I would not
otherwise be able to love.

A Revival of Love

I now pray that millions of Christians throughout the
world will begin to love by faith. When this happens, I believe
revival will sweep the world, and the floodgates will open for
the fulfillment of the Great Commission, as happened in the
early church.

Love was the major result of the Holy Spirit's work in the first-century church. It was said of the early Christians, "How they love one another." Most certainly this supernatural love drew multitudes of non-believers into the kingdom, and thus the gospel began spreading to the then-known world.

Characteristics of the Agape *Person*

God calls us to love supernaturally — to be *agape* persons — so that we might become more effective witnesses for the Lord Jesus Christ. He wants us to become involved in building other *agape* persons through discipling in an ongoing movement of "spiritual multiplication" that will help to change the world for Christ.

As this kind of spiritual maturity takes place in our Christian faith, a number of characteristics will become noticeable realities in our lives. These characteristics, which are manifestations of the Holy Spirit at work in us, enable us to love supernaturally.

This list is a foundational part of our international training curriculum which has been developed under the leadership of Kent Hutcheson, as we have worked with our directors throughout the world. Kent and his wife, Diane, have helped to train many thousands of staff, students and laymen around the world.

Faith. The *agape* person is consistently aware of the character of the Triune God — one God manifest in three persons: Father, Son and Holy Spirit. He draws upon the infinite resources of God by faith in order to live the Christian life. He understands that faith is his response to all that God is and all that He promises to those who trust and obey Him.

Stewardship. The *agape* person allows Christ to be Lord of every area of his life — his mind, body, relationships, talents and material possessions. He recognizes that all which he has is ultimately a gift of God, and he considers himself a responsible steward of these blessings.

Power. The *agape* person invites and encourages the Holy Spirit, who indwells him, to control his daily life increasingly. Thus, he is becoming more and more in character like our Lord Jesus Christ.

Prayer. The *agape* person — following the example of our Lord, the disciples and Christian leaders throughout the centuries — places a special priority on prayer and his daily communication with God. He realizes that God delights in his fellowship, desires his worship and welcomes his requests.

Obedience. The *agape* person seeks to obey God daily. As he understands the commands and desires of God, he is willing to submit to them and make them his own desires. He realizes that obedience to his heavenly Father involves submission to those who are placed in authority over him.

Direction. The *agape* person depends on the Word of God for direction and guidance in every circumstance. He accepts the Bible as his final authority — his source of knowledge about God, others and himself.

Action. The *agape* person views his life as an opportunity to serve his Lord actively. He is consistently winning others to Christ, helping to build and disciple them in their faith and sending them forth as spiritual multipliers to win and build others for the Savior. His purpose is to live for Christ in his own sphere of influence, help to fulfill the Great Commission in his generation and thus help to change the world.

Vision. The *agape* person views the world, its problems, needs and opportunities from God's perspective. His prayer is, "Lord Jesus, if You were I, what would You be doing and planning in the power of the Holy Spirit?" He acknowledges that his talents, abilities and dreams are a gift from God and offers them back to the Lord Jesus Christ, trusting Him for their fulfillment.

Leadership. The *agape* person is a leader in the particular area where God has placed him. As such, he consistently encourages others to Christian commitment and Spirit-controlled action, and works to mobilize them in an ongoing movement to help fulfill the Great Commission.

Fellowship. The *agape* person enjoys fellowship with God's people worldwide. He loves the church, involves himself in it and supports its efforts to help fulfill the Great Commission.

Love. Finally, the *agape* person experiences the unconditional, supernatural love of God in his daily life and expresses that same quality of love in meaningful ways to family, friends, acquaintances and strangers — believers and non-believers alike.

The characteristics and life-style of the *agape* person are supernatural. Only the supernatural person of the Lord Jesus Christ can live such a life — which He wants to do in and through every believer.

An International Incident

Bailey Marks, our director of affairs for the continent of Asia, has influenced millions of Asians for Christ through his leadership of our Asian staff. He has learned to "love supernaturally" and is seeing the impact of this truth multiplied all over that vast continent.

One opportunity to share the concept of loving by faith came to Bailey as he was riding on a bus in the Philippine Islands and began a conversation with the young man in the seat next to him. Their conversation soon led to spiritual topics, and Bailey began sharing the Four Spiritual Laws with his fellow passenger, named Jerry. As they talked about the contents of the booklet, Jerry expressed a desire to receive Jesus Christ as his Savior. They prayed together, and the young man invited Christ into his life.

As they talked further, Bailey realized his friend was having one difficulty — he didn't understand that *all,* not just some, of his sins had been forgiven, and that he now had eternal life.

So, to clarify the all-important truth that at salvation sins are forgiven entirely, Bailey decided to use the illustration of a father-son relationship. "Jerry, have you ever put your arm around your father and told him how much you love him?" Bailey asked.

"No," Jerry said, "I haven't. And if I did, he wouldn't believe me."

Then Bailey, knowing Jerry's father was on the bus, suggested, "We're coming to a rest stop in a few minutes. When we get off the bus, why don't you try it?" They got off the bus, and Bailey walked inside a restaurant near the rest stop.

Moment of Decision

A few minutes later, Jerry came into the restaurant with his father and introduced him to Bailey. As the trio climbed aboard the bus, Jerry asked Bailey to sit next to his father.

"I want you to tell him what you told me this morning," he said.

Soon the father, whose name was Pat, had prayed, asking Jesus Christ to be his Savior, and a moment after he had finished praying the prayer, he looked up at Bailey.

"Now I know why Jerry said what he did a little while ago," he said.

Bailey asked, "What did Jerry say to you?"

Pat answered, "When we got off the bus, he told me, 'Papa, I want you to know that I love you more than anything else in the world.' "

"What did you say to him?" Bailey asked.

"My response was not very nice."

Bailey said, "Pat, what do you think Jerry would do if you put your arm around him and said, 'Son, I love you so much'?"

Pat thought a moment, and then apparently picturing such a scene in his mind, smiled, "I would like to do that." Then Pat looked over at Bailey, "Do you believe in praying for other people?" he asked. At that point, the two men paused together and prayed for a new life and a new relationship for the once-estranged father and son.

When the bus arrived at Baguio City, Bailey's destination, Pat and Jerry disembarked also. When they stepped off the bus, Pat put his arms around his son and said, "Jerry, I want you to know how much I love you."

Bailey remarks today that one of his most beautiful memories is of this father and son, with tears streaming down their faces, united together in the love of Christ.

Are you experiencing this supernatural love in your life for God, for others, for yourself, for your enemies? Christ commands in John 15:12 that we love one another, just as He loves us. And remember, with every command which God has given to us, He has given us either definite or implied promises that He will enable us to obey it.

Why not make a list of those whom you are having difficulty loving as God loves? Included in this list might be your husband or your wife, your parents or your children. The list might include a neighbor or co-worker who is spreading hurtful rumors about you. Or a family member who is lacking in sensitivity toward other family members. Or, perhaps, a close relationship has just been broken, and you are fighting feelings of resentment toward the other person.

Begin today to love them supernaturally and unconditionally, by faith, as an act of the will. Make this a lifetime practice, a way of life. In this way, you will begin the great adventure of loving supernaturally.

CHAPTER TEN

How to Give Supernaturally

Giving supernaturally is one of the greatest privileges and blessings of the Christian life. Again and again God has promised us prosperity and abundance as we give of the riches which He has entrusted to us.

One of the greatest discoveries that I have made in my adventuresome walk with God has been the privilege of giving supernaturally, as I've learned the importance of "seeking first the kingdom of God"[1] and "laying up treasures in heaven."[2]

Total Commitment

As I have already shared, my wife, Vonette, and I made a total commitment of our lives to Christ in 1951, including the giving of our finances and all material possessions to Him. Since that time, on thousands of occasions, we have experienced the faithfulness of God to meet our every need "superabundantly" above and beyond our fondest hopes and desires.[3]

Though as a result of our commitment to Christ, we own very little of this world's goods, we have always enjoyed the "best" of everything — without asking for it. For example, in the last 28 years since our decision to surrender our lives and material possessions to Christ, the five homes we have had have been as nice as or nicer than anything we might have chosen had I been a millionaire — yet we have never actually sought to live luxuriously.

The homes have been chosen on the basis of their abilities to contribute to a more fruitful ministry for our Lord. We have rented each home on terms which we could afford on our modest income. The car which we use for personal and Campus Crusade ministry is provided by a long-time dear friend, who has also discovered the supernatural law of giving and is equally blessed of God.

God has provided all our needs and our desires. Though we own nothing apart from a few personal effects and have no savings for the future, I cannot think of a single thing that

Vonette and I want that we do not have — except more finances and other blessings of God to pass on to others.

Living by Giving

If all Christians could know and apply the biblical principles of this incredible, supernatural way of living by "giving and receiving," not only would they be personally blessed, but also vast sums of money and other valuable resources would suddenly be released to help fulfill the Great Commission immediately, and to help meet the physical needs of the poor, the sick and the illiterate of the world. In fact, so many billions of dollars would be converted into changed lives by the power of the risen Christ that the entire course of history would be dramatically changed.

We, as Christians, surely have the manpower, the technology, the strategies, the materials — everything that is needed to saturate the entire world for Christ except money — money which is still in the hands of Christians who have not yet discovered the privilege and adventure of giving supernaturally.

In defining supernatural giving, I would contrast using money primarily for personal or selfish motives with "supernatural giving," which is taking God at His Word and giving generously. It is believing He will supply and therefore investing in the various legitimate causes which honor and glorify Him. It is meeting, as a representative of Christ, the physical and spiritual needs of others. When we give supernaturally, we experience the fulfillment of God's promise that we will reap more than we sow.

Rich and Poor Alike

The law of supernatural, Spirit-directed giving applies both to the poor and the rich — those who can only give the "widow's mite" and those who have the ability to give millions to the cause of Christ. God desires to bless His children abundantly and promises to do so, if only we will demonstrate faith in Him through trust and obedience to Him. But, if we fail to trust and obey, we will not only miss the greatest blessings of God but also may actually experience the chastening of God.

Consider His word to Judah and Jerusalem, which is also applicable to us as His children today: "Will a man rob God?

Surely not! And yet you have robbed Me! . . . You have robbed Me of the tithes and offerings due to Me. And so the awesome curse of God is cursing you, for your whole nation has been robbing Me. Bring all the tithes into the storehouse so that there will be food enough in My Temple; if you do, I will open up the windows of heaven for you and pour out a blessing so great you won't have room enough to take it in!"[4]

Shortly after the beginning of the Here's Life, World campaign, Vonette and I began devoting most of our time to helping launch campaigns in many cities on most continents. During 1977 and 1978 we visited 46 countries on almost all continents and met with staff and Christian leaders from 75 countries. Wherever we went we were faced with urgent financial needs.

Since most of the Christian wealth of the world, an estimated 80%, is in the hands of Christians in the United States and Canada, it became obvious that God wanted us to help Christians in other countries to disciple and evangelize their own people. We concluded that the most important thing which we can do to help is to encourage Christians whom God has blessed so abundantly to provide money, materials, training and prayer for those in other lands who have so little.

Investing Now, Not Later

Since God wants to bless you in a special way, He also wants you to invest the material resources which He has entrusted to you *while you are alive* to help reach the world for Christ.

When I explained to a group of executives how the concept of investing while they are still alive can influence their gifts' maximum use for the glory of God, a very successful businessman responded with great enthusiasm, "I have never heard that truth explained before. I've been reared in the church, I love the Lord and I have given generously to various Christian causes. I had always considered that God's part of the money I made was a tithe, which I gave gladly, and the rest was mine. Now I see that it all belongs to God, and He has made me a steward of His blessings to be invested for Him while I am still alive."

Recently, a friend shared this heart-warming story. He had been appointed the executor of a sizeable estate. This meant that he would be responsible, in this particular case, to give the money away after the person died. He encouraged the person, who was a devout Christian and quite elderly, to give the money away while she was still alive and could observe first-hand the benefits of her investments.

They prayed together, and with his counsel and the help of others, she began to write checks to many different worthy Christian projects — missionaries, struggling new churches, mission organizations, Christian schools, etc. The results were predictable. She obeyed God, and He blessed her in a way she had never known. Never had Christ been so real to her and never had she been so excited about Him and the privilege of serving Him.

Treasures in Heaven

Many Christians miss the special blessing of God because they do not obey our Lord's commands. One of the most important commands is found in Matthew 6, "Don't store up treasures here on earth where they can erode away or may be stolen. Store them in heaven where they will never lose their value, and are safe from thieves. If your profits are in heaven your heart will be there too. . . . You cannot serve two masters: God and money. For you will hate one and love the other, or else the other way around."[5]

Jesus Christ gave this command for our good. If we store up treasures, we soon take on the appearance of the world through selfish desires, ceasing to reflect His purpose and glory.

Jesus then admonishes us not to worry about such things as food, drink and clothes or our future security — if God takes care of the birds of the air and the flowers of the field, how much more will He take care of us. We are far more valuable to Him than they are.[6] Jesus promises to be our total sufficiency if we only allow Him to be.

God-given Abilities . . .

God's Word teaches us that He gives abilities to each of His children in order for them to do certain things well. Some Christians are blessed with the ability to lead, others to preach and teach, and still others to perform services of help or mercy.

God has given each person a variety of abilities; He expects good stewardship of us in the use of these abilities. Just as a steward is responsible for another's management and household, each Christian is responsible for using his abilities to meet needs of the Body of Christ.

We are also told that it is the same Holy Spirit who is the source of all such special abilities.[7] He does so to display "God's power through each of us as a means of helping the entire church."[8]

... God-given Responsibilities

One responsibility which many Christians often overlook as being divinely ordained is the ability to accumulate wealth and distribute it in accordance with God's plan. God's inspired Word says, "Always remember that it is the Lord your God who gives you power to become rich. . . ."[9]

This truth is stated again in Romans 12:8, "If God has given you money, be generous in helping others with it" (Living). Notice there is no reference to the amount, only to the responsibility of wisely handling the money one receives.

The individual who possesses material blessings from God and the ability to acquire even more but who does not use them properly is just as disobedient as the individual who fails to utilize any other God-given ability. And disobedience in the area of financial stewardship will produce the same consequences as any other area where God's commands are clear but are not kept: guilt, frustration and insecurity. Thus, it is not uncommon for Christians who have disobeyed God in the area of finances to be apprehensive about losing their wealth or what they have accumulated. They also are usually frustrated, confused and unfulfilled in other ways because of their disobedience.

I think of one woman, a Christian, worth many millions of dollars, who panicked when the stock market dropped and she lost almost one million dollars. Even though she had many millions in reserve, she was filled with apprehension and fear that she would die a pauper. She had never discovered the adventure and freedom of "giving and receiving" in a trust relationship with God.

Many References to Giving

The principles of giving are found throughout the whole of Scripture, beginning in Genesis 1, where God gave of His very being to create the universe, and continues through the Book of Revelation. There are over seven hundred references to giving in the Bible. The New Testament has more to say about giving than about the return of Christ, and Jesus speaks about stewardship and giving as much as, if not more than, any other subject.

Giving began with God Himself. His ultimate expression of giving His love for lost man was when He gave His only begotten Son that we might have eternal life. Christ in turn gave His life by dying for our sins so that we could personally relate to God the Father. God continues to give to us of Himself — love, forgiveness, peace, purpose and a power to live full, meaningful lives. God is the source of all life and continues to provide us with food, air, water, shelter and clothing, which we often take for granted.

Today most Christians have been influenced by the world system of "getting" rather than God's plan of "giving." Secular views have been adopted by most Christians, views expressed in statements such as, "Money is the key to happiness," "Look out for yourself — if you don't no one else will," and "Get what you can, while you can, and can what you get." As a result, most Christians are frustrated and confused. They have been deceived by the enemy of our souls and have missed the blessings of God.

For instance, one Christian father, following the example of the world, set up a large trust for his children and was surprised and disappointed that one of them had no incentive to work. Upon insisting that the child get a job, the response was, "Why should I work? I have all the income I'll ever need for the rest of my life from the trust you set up."

Problem-solving

Another godly couple told me of their concern that their considerable wealth, which they had accumulated to leave for their daughter, was now in jeopardy, for their daughter had married an atheist who would not even allow their grandchildren to attend Sunday school.

"What shall we do?" they inquired. "This is money which God has given us, and we were leaving it behind so that our daughter and her family would be well cared for."

I responded, "Since God has enabled you to make and save a large sum of money, He desires you to be a wise steward of that which He has entrusted to your care. After you have made reasonable provision for your family, I would suggest that you investigate various ministries for Christ which are committed to helping fulfill the Great Commission. Those ministries that are being used of God to win and disciple others for Christ deserve your support."

God Is Faithful

Just as I was writing this chapter, a long-distance telephone call came from a businessman, a long-time friend who loves the Lord and who has experienced the exciting reality of "living by giving."

It was as though God Himself arranged the call to underline the point which I am making.

My friend called to tell me how excited he was over the way God was blessing his new business venture and that he had decided to give all the business' profits toward helping to reach the world for Christ.

"I am sending $50,000 for Here's Life in Asia," he said. "And there will be much more later. I don't want to invest in buildings. I want to invest this money where it will be used immediately to win and disciple people for Christ."

Think of the challenge that awaits millions of Christians when they discover how to give supernaturally from the material blessings which they have already accumulated, or, as in the case of my friend, while they are still receiving them. The return on their investments will accomplish much for the glory of God and demonstrate good stewardship of God's financial blessings, even while they are living.

Please understand that this principle applies to Christians of modest means as well as individuals of great wealth. Just as every businessman knows his success depends upon his ability to make good investments which will result in the largest possible dividend, so should it be with our spiritual investments. *Every* Christian should think in terms of how he can give the most of what God has entrusted to him to help win and disciple the largest possible number of people for Christ and bring them into the fellowship of the church.

The Greatest Privilege

The greatest privilege in the life of the Christian is to glorify God. The Westminster Confession of Faith puts it this way: "The chief end of man is to glorify God and to enjoy Him forever." As I mentioned earlier, each gift from God, including the ability to make money, is entrusted to the believer to be used for the glory of God.

Man is so created that he finds his maximum fulfillment only when he is living a life of faith and obedience to God. God means for each gift He gives to be maximized here on earth as a contribution to the fulfillment of His purpose, which is for all men to have a chance to hear the good news of the gospel.

Those, for instance, to whom have been given the skills of effective preaching and teaching of the Word of God are expected to utilize these skills to the fullest in their lifetimes. They cannot bequeath their abilities to their children. Unfortunately, most people do not realize that this is equally true for those whom God has blessed with the ability to make and accumulate wealth.

The prophet Haggai records God's admonition, "You hope for much but get so little. And when you bring it home, I blow it away — it doesn't last at all. Why? Because My Temple lies in ruins and you don't care. Your only concern is your own fine homes. That is why I am holding back the rains from heaven and giving you such scant crops."[10]

Ultimately, the Christian who possesses wealth but does not recognize his accountability to God is bound to suffer such chastening and even may, in time, cease to prosper. On the other hand, blessings will surely come to those who obey God by properly investing their God-given funds to the maximum for His glory.

But the blessings of God are showered abundantly upon all those who trust and obey the Lord in using whatever they receive from God.

Responsibility for the Family

Sometimes the question is raised regarding how much money one should give to his family and how much to God.

Often, wealthy Christians leave vast estates for their children, and observers wonder why both end up being miserable. It is because the parents have disobeyed God's command to "lay up treasures in heaven." They have failed to invest for His glory, while they are living, that which God has entrusted to them.

I would want to emphasize strongly, however, that the Scriptures tell us that whoever does not care for his own family is "worse than an infidel."[11] Obviously, God wants us to care for our spouses and children, primarily by helping them to love the Lord Jesus Christ and to maximize their ability to earn wealth for God's glory, or to serve the Lord in some other way.

A friend whom God has blessed very generously has arranged for each child to receive a certain amount of money each year for several years with the understanding that the money really belongs to the Lord and they are to invest it for Him and His kingdom. He and his wife will invest the rest of their sizeable estate for the Lord where they believe it will accomplish the most for the glory of God.

How About the "Average" Person?

Some of you may be saying, "Your counsel is mostly to individuals who have accumulated some degree of this world's wealth. But what counsel can you give to me? I own very little of this world's goods. All I have is my monthly paycheck out of which I must pay my rent, car payments, food, clothing, insurance, medical and other expenses.

"How am I to respond to Christ's command to lay up treasures in heaven? How can I be a part of helping to fulfill the Great Commission?"

First of all, you must ask God to tell you what to do.

Second, look for a project which you can support monthly, if only modestly, in addition to your commitment to your local church.

As your faith in God's love and trustworthiness grows, prayerfully make a faith promise pledge that is greater than you are capable of fulfilling according to your present income. Prayerfully expect God to honor this expression of your faith in Him and your obedience to His command to help fulfill the

Great Commission. If He so desires, He will provide you with the necessary funds to meet your faith promise pledge.

As someone has wisely put it, we should recognize that everything over which we have stewardship belongs to God — not to ourselves. "It is not how much we give to God out of what belongs to us but how much we keep for ourselves out of that which belongs to God."

In His Sermon on the Mount, Jesus emphasizes the importance and results of obedience. "Your Heavenly Father already knows perfectly well what you need and He will give it to you if you give Him first place in your life and live as He wants you to."[12]

Perhaps you are in between those who possess considerable wealth and those who live from paycheck to paycheck. You are asking, "What should I do with the profits from my investments?"

A friend came for counsel concerning his financial investments for the Lord. "The Lord has blessed me with a steady income," he said, "but I am not wealthy. Over the last two years one of our investments has resulted in an additional income of $10,000. I'm not sure whether we should give all of this to the Lord now, tithe on it, or invest it with the possibility of making additional profits for the Lord.

"At what point," he continued, "do you continue to invest the money you make? How much should you keep as seed money, in order to make more for the Lord?"

It seems to me that the principles might be:
1. Maintain the same standard of living you have now.
2. Possibly determine some investments where *all* profits will go to the Lord. See how much money you can make for Him!
3. Seriously determine the greatest opportunity for the advancement of the gospel, against which you can evaluate every personal expenditure.
4. Ask the Lord how much above the tithe on profits He wants you to give. Perhaps He will want you to give it all. Perhaps only a portion.

"Borrowing for the Kingdom"

In addition, you might consider "borrowing for the kingdom." Most successful business people look for sound business opportunities that are likely to bring a good return on their investment. When they find something that is especially promising, they do not hesitate to borrow money, even large sums, against their assets to invest. The same can apply in the spiritual realm.

For example, one friend sold a house to finance Here's Life, Bangkok. The $75,000 represented most of his life's savings, but thousands of people were introduced to Christ. Here's Life campaigns are now being held in several cities of Thailand. His investment financed most of the campaign in Bangkok and without his help it, too, would have been cancelled. As a result, he has had a personal investment in every person reached for Christ directly or indirectly through the money which he gave.

The Principle of Sowing and Reaping

There is a law of God that promises that the more we sow the more we reap. Jesus said, ". . . Anyone who gives up his home, brothers, sisters, father, mother, wife, children or property, to follow Me, shall receive a hundred times as much in return, and shall have eternal life."[13] How could anyone *lose* on such a transaction?

Whatever you give up to follow Jesus will be returned to you a hundredfold — plus eternal life. This is a promise from our Lord Himself, and He does not lie. We can, with all certainty, expect the fulfillment of that promise when we trust and obey God.

From my own commitment made nearly 30 years ago, I can tell you that this promise is true. From my observations after having spoken with literally hundreds of Christian leaders around the world, as well as having observed the thousands whom I have counseled, I do not know of anyone who would say that this spiritual law has not been true in his life. Many Christians know that law intellectually, but they do not apply it.

Giving Cheerfully

Not only does God want us to "sow" generously, but He loves a "*cheerful* giver."[14] The Greek work for "cheerful" is *hilaros,* from which we get the word "hilarious." Supernatural, Spirit-directed giving is giving with anticipation, excitement, joy, praise and even laughter. A hilarious giver has discovered the truth of Acts 20:33, "It is more blessed to give than to receive." Learn to give cheerfully and with joyful trust that the many promises of God which we have reviewed will become your experience.

Time Is Running Out

The time to give is now. The powerful tide of atheism, secular humanism, materialism, communism and other evils are threatening to engulf the world. From the human perspective, on the basis of what I see and hear, I could be very pessimistic about the future freedom of mankind, for we are well within the reality of being plunged into another thousand years or more of dark ages.

I am more optimistic, however, not on the basis of what I see and hear, but on the basis of what I believe God is saying to my heart and what I am observing that He is doing throughout the world, because I am constantly reminded and assured, ". . . Greater is He that is in you, than he that is in the world."[15]

But it is sobering to realize that, unless those of us who care for the freedom of man and the kingdom of God are willing to pay whatever price is necessary in terms of time and talent and treasure, all could be lost.

The fortunes that have been accumulated, the estates that have been built, the trusts that have been set up for families, the foundations that are meant to perpetuate family names, all will be gone and all will be lost. The loss will be not only the accumulated wealth but also, more important, freedom itself. Possibly, for millions, it could mean death. Yet, if enough of us are willing to trust and obey our Lord and His command, we can be assured of victory as we are willing to unite in one great, committed thrust for the glory and praise of God.

As Edmund Burke once said, "All that is needed for evil to triumph is that good men do nothing." May I encourage you to begin to prayerfully evaluate various opportunities to win and disciple others for Christ — investing your God-given treasure now where it will accomplish the most for the glory of God by helping to fulfill the Great Commission.

What Are "Good Men" to Do?

Since we know by God's own promise that blessings will surely come to those who obey Him by properly investing their God-given funds, I would like to suggest that you keep the following things in mind as you seek supernaturally to become a better steward.

First, remember that everything actually belongs to God, and we are His stewards here on earth.

Second, God does not want us to hoard His blessings. If you and I and Christians everywhere obey our Lord's command to lay up treasures in heaven — to invest His financial blessings while we are still alive, knowing that all we possess is a gift of God and that we are accountable to Him for the way we spend it, great sums of money will be released to be invested in the advancement of His kingdom. As a result, hundreds of millions of people will be reached for Christ, and the Great Commission will be fulfilled.

Third, there is the law of God, "As you sow, you reap." What you harvest and the amount you harvest is determined by what you sow and the amount you sow. The individual Christian who keeps his financial priorities straight will be assured of God's blessings. All of his needs will be met, according to Matthew 6:33.

Fourth, we should be willing to give more than a tithe of our current income — God may lead us to give of our savings and accumulated wealth beyond the amount needed to meet the reasonable needs of our family and business. We should prayerfully seek God's wisdom concerning the giving of, or borrowing against, property, stocks and bonds to help win and disciple others for Christ in other countries.

Fifth, we should learn to give supernaturally by faith. Ask God to enable you to give beyond what you are capable of giving. This is one of the most exciting and rewarding ways to invest for Christ and His kingdom.

From our personal account, Vonette and I have pledged to give to foreign national ministries more than we keep for our own salaries.

Sixth, we are to give cheerfully — recognizing that we are called to be obedient, faithful stewards of all that God has entrusted to us — not how much we give to God from that which belongs to us but how much we keep for ourselves of that which belongs to God.

Seventh, we give out of a sense of urgency, mindful that our investments can help build a better world. Because of growing worldwide problems, we must do all we can to help now before it is too late. If ever we plan to do anything for Christ and His kingdom, we must do it now.

Finally — and perhaps most important — the individual who obeys God in this area of finances as in other areas will experience a closer and more vital personal walk with Him, unhampered by disobedience.

God Is the Author of Every Perfect Gift

God is original with each of us, and so I cannot suggest what your personal life-style should be. But let each of us see to it, for the glory of God and our own personal blessing, that we seek first His kingdom and recognize that everything we have comes from Him. Most of all, let us always remember that we are to use for His glory the money which He entrusts to us no less diligently than His gifts of time and talent.

In actuality, we "own" nothing. Everything belongs to God, and we have use of material possessions for only a brief moment of time while we are here on this earth.

God is waiting to bless His children supernaturally. Yet, He cannot bless us if we disobey Him. I pray that every person who reads these truths from God's Word concerning stewardship will discover the supernatural joy and blessing of faithful stewardship.

CHAPTER ELEVEN

How to Experience the Supernatural Will of God

One of the marks of a Spirit-filled Christian is that his life is characterized by a new sense of purpose; he has a desire, not for complacency, but for his life to have meaning and direction. He has an "eternal perspective" toward his life and accomplishments.

Some years ago, a young college graduate came to me for counsel concerning God's will for his life. "How can I know what God wants me to do?" he asked.

Briefly, I explained a helpful approach to knowing the will of God: to follow what I have chosen to call the "sound mind principle of Scripture."

In less than an hour, by following the suggestions contained in this principle, the young man discovered what he had been seeking for years. He discovered not only the work which God wanted him to do but also the place and manner in which he was to fulfill his work. Today he is serving Christ as a missionary in Africa, where he and his wife are touching the lives of thousands throughout the entire continent.

The Sound Mind Principle

What is this "sound mind principle"? We are told in II Timothy, "God hath not given us the spirit of fear; but of power, and of love and of a sound mind."[1]

The sound mind to which this verse refers means a well-balanced mind — a mind that is under the control of the Holy Spirit. It is a mind "remade" in the manner of Paul's description of Romans 12: "And so, dear brothers, I plead with you to give your bodies to God. Let them be a living sacrifice, holy — the kind He can accept. . . . Don't copy the behavior and customs of this world, but be a new and different person with a fresh newness in all you do and think. Then you will learn from your own experience how His ways will really satisfy you."[2]

There is a vast difference between the inclination of the natural or carnal man to use "common sense" and that of a spiritual man to follow the sound mind principle, which is based on God's Word. One depends upon man's limited understanding without benefit of God's wisdom and power; the latter, having the mind of Christ, receives wisdom and guidance from God and His inspired Word moment by moment through faith.

Are your decisions as a Christian based upon unpredictable emotions and chance circumstances? Or do you make your decisions according to Scripture's sound mind guidelines?

Through the years, as I have counseled with many Christians, one of the questions most frequently asked has been, "How can I know the will of God for my life?" Inevitably, the majority of Christians who come for counsel are looking for some dramatic or cataclysmic revelation from God by which they will know His plans.

Without minimizing the importance of feelings (which Jesus promised would come as a result of obedience),[3] more emphasis needs to be placed upon the importance of the sound mind which God has given us. Multitudes of sincere Christians are wasting their lives, and are spiritually immobile and impotent, as they wait for some unusual or dramatic word from God.

Faith Is the Key

But a Christian who has yielded his life fully to Christ can be assured of Spirit-directed reasoning and a balanced, disciplined mind. God has promised to give His children wisdom simply for the asking — if we ask in faith.[4] He has also promised we can know with "settled and absolute assurance" that when we pray according to His will, He will always hear and grant our petitions.[5]

Since the Christian is to live by faith — and faith comes through an understanding of the Word of God — it is impossible to overemphasize the importance of the Scriptures in the lives of those who would know and do the will of God.

The only truly happy, fulfilled, fruitful life is that which is lived in the perfect will of God. If you would like to know the will of God for your life according to the sound mind principle of Scripture, may I suggest that you consider these questions:

"Why did Jesus come?" The answer: He came to "seek and save the lost."[6] Then, ask yourself, "What is the greatest experience of my life?" If you are a Christian, your answer will quite obviously be: "To know Christ personally as my Savior and Lord." Finally, "What is the greatest thing that I can do to help others?" The answer is again obvious: "Introduce them to Christ."

Jesus came to seek and to save the lost, and every Christian is under divine orders to be a faithful witness for Christ. Jesus said, "My true disciples produce bountiful harvests. This brings great glory to My Father."[7] So it follows that the most important thing I can possibly do as a Christian is to allow the Lord Jesus Christ in all of His resurrection power to have complete, unhindered control of my life. Otherwise, He cannot continue seeking and saving the lost through me.

Total Availability

Thus, every sincere Christian will want to make his God-given time, talents and treasure available to Christ so that his fullest potential will be realized for His kingdom. For one Christian, the talent which God has given him may be prophetic preaching, evangelism or teaching; for another, it may be business; for another, the ministry or missions; for still another, homemaker — or whatever ability or gift God might have given one (as expressed in Romans 12, I Corinthians 12 and 14, and Ephesians 4).

As you evaluate what God has given you in relation to your training, personality and other qualities, may I suggest that you take a sheet of paper and make a list of the most logical ways through which your life can be used to accomplish the most for the glory of God. Your list may include some or all of the following: business, teaching, medicine, law, media, ministry and missions. You may wish to add to this list.

With the desire to put His will above all else, list the pros and cons of each opportunity. Where or how, according to the sound mind principle, can the Lord Jesus Christ through your yielded life accomplish the most in continuing His great ministry of "seeking and saving the lost"?

Like my young friend, you will find that such a procedure will inevitably result in positive actions leading to God's perfect will for your life. But note a word of caution: the sound mind principle is not valid unless certain factors exist.

First, breathe spiritually if necessary — exhale by confessing your sins. There must be no unconfessed sin in your life. Claiming the promise of I John 1:9 takes care of that, "If we confess our sins, God is faithful and just to forgive us our sins and to cleanse us from all unrighteousness."

A Yielded Life

Second, inhale — appropriate the filling of the Holy Spirit by faith. Your life must be fully dedicated to Christ, according to Romans 12:1,2, and you must be filled with the Holy Spirit in obedience to the command of Ephesians 5:18, and the promise of I John 5:14,15. As I have mentioned previously, we are filled and controlled by the Spirit through faith, just as we receive our salvation as a gift of God by faith.

Finally, in order to know the will of God, you must walk in the Spirit (abide in Christ) moment by moment. Place your faith in the trustworthiness of God with the confidence that the Lord is directing and will continue to direct your life according to His promise that the "steps of a good man are ordered of the Lord."[8] Paul tells us in Colossians that just as we have received Christ by faith, so we must walk in Him by faith.[9]

How do you walk by faith? By placing your complete trust in God and His inspired Word. You must go on walking by faith. Remember, "that which is not of faith is sin,"[10] and "the just shall live by faith."[11] Indeed, "without faith it is impossible to please Him."[12] Faith is the basis of the Christian life and therefore must be the basis of our decisions.

The counsel of other Christians should also be prayerfully considered, especially that of mature, Spirit-controlled Christians who know the Word of God and who are able to relate the proper use of Scripture to your need. However, care should be taken not to make the counsel of others a "crutch." Learn to go to God and His Word for help instead of constantly depending on others.

Although God often speaks to us through other Christians, we are admonished to place our trust in Him. In Psalms 37 we are told to delight ourselves in the Lord, and He will give us the desires of our hearts, to commit our ways to the Lord, to trust Him and He will bring it to pass.

Also, in Proverbs 3 we read, "Trust in the Lord with all thine heart; and lean not unto thine own understanding. In all thy ways acknowledge Him, and He shall direct thy paths."[13]

God never contradicts Himself. He never leads us to do anything contrary to the commands of His Word, for according to Philippians 2:13, "It is God who is at work within you, giving you the will and power to achieve His purpose" (Phillips).

Through the centuries, sincere religious men have suggested spiritual "formulas" for discovering the will of God. Some are valid, but others are unscriptural and misleading.

For example, a young seminary graduate came to see me while he was investigating various possibilities of Christian service. In particular, he had come to discuss the ministry of Campus Crusade. I asked him, "In what way do you expect God to reveal His place of service for you?"

He replied, "I am following the 'closed-door' policy. A few months ago I began to investigate several opportunities for Christian service. The Lord has now closed the door on all but two, one of which is Campus Crusade. If the door to accept a call to a particular church closes, I will know that God wants me in Campus Crusade."

Many sincere Christians follow this method but often with most unsatisfactory and frustrating consequences. Don't misunderstand. God may — and often does — close doors in the life of every active, Spirit-controlled Christian. Certainly this was true in the experience of the apostle Paul. We read in Acts 16:6-11 that he was forbidden by the Spirit to go into Bithynia because God wanted him in Macedonia.

My reference to closed door policies does not preclude such experiences, but refers to a careless "hit or miss" attitude without the careful evaluation of all the issues. This approach is illogical because it allows elements of chance to influence a decision rather than a careful, intelligent, prayerful evaluation of all the factors involved. Further, it is unscriptural in that it fails to employ the God-given faculties of reason that are controlled by the Holy Spirit.

The closed-door policy is also in error because it seeks God's will through the process of elimination rather than seeking God's best first. It should be understood that true faith is established on the basis of fact. Therefore, vital faith in God is emphasized rather than minimized through employing Spirit-controlled reason.

Faith Is Not "Blind"

In making decisions, some sincere Christians rely almost entirely upon impressions or "spiritual hunches," fearful that if they use their mental faculties they will not exercise adequate faith and thus will grieve the Holy Spirit. Actually, the opposite is true.

There are those who assume that a door has been closed simply because of difficulties which have been encountered. Yet, experience has taught, and Scripture confirms, that God's richest blessings often follow periods of greatest testing. This might include financial needs, loss of health, objection of loved ones and criticism of fellow Christians.

God's blessings are promised only to those who are obedient, who keep on trusting and working in the power of the Holy Spirit, who demonstrate their faith in God's faithfulness. We must never forget that the apparent defeat of the cross was followed by the victory of the resurrection.

God's will is revealed in (1) the authority of Scripture, (2) providential circumstances, (3) conviction based upon reason and (4) impressions of the Holy Spirit upon our minds.

Discernment Needed

Indeed, you must know the source of leading before responding to it. Sometimes what appears to be the leading of the Spirit may not be from God at all but from "the rulers of the darkness of this world." Satan and his helpers often disguise themselves as "angels of light"[14] by performing miracles, signs and foretelling events. Remember, the enemy of our souls is the master counterfeiter. Always compare impressions with the Scriptures.

Remember also that just as turning the steering wheel of an automobile does not alter its direction unless the car is moving, so God cannot direct our lives unless we are moving for Him.

I challenge you to begin employing the sound mind principle today in all your relationships — with husband or wife, parents or children, and with all your friends and neighbors. Apply it to the investment of your time, your talents and your treasure; for this principle applies to everything you do in this life.

Every Christian should take spiritual inventory regularly by asking himself these questions: Is my time being invested in such a way that the largest possible number of people are being reached and discipled for Christ? Are my talents being invested to the fullest so that the largest possible number of people are being reached and discipled for Christ? Is my money (my treasure) being invested in such a way as to reach and disciple the greatest number of people for Christ?

Every Christian is admonished to be a good steward of his God-given abilities and possessions. Therefore, these investments must not be dictated by tradition, habit or emotions. Every investment of your time, energy and finances should be determined by the direction and principles of God's Word.

Further, every Christian is to be a witness for Christ. Witnessing is simply an act of obedience for which one need not possess any special gift of evangelism. Normal day-to-day contacts providing opportunities to witness for Christ are greatly enhanced by prayer. An obedient Christian will pray for daily opportunities to make Christ known through personal contacts, church calling or letter writing.

God Is Not Limited

Two of the most radiant, effective and fruitful Christians whom I have ever known were both invalids who, though in constant pain, bore a powerful witness for Christ to all — stranger and friend alike. "That which is most on our hearts will be most on our lips" was demonstrated in their lives.

Likewise, a careful evaluation should be given to determine if God may not have a better position in mind for us. Again, the sound mind principle applies.

For example, an executive who is "successful" in business but unfulfilled should employ the sound mind principle to determine if his God-given time, talent and treasure are being maximized for His glory. Or, a secretary in a secular organization may feel she has limited opportunity to make her life count for the Lord; thus, God may want such secretarial talent used in a Christian organization.

A person should be very careful, however, not to run from what appears to be a difficult assignment. A careful appraisal of one's present responsibilities, along with this new understanding of God's leading, may well reveal a great potential for Christ.

It just so happens that I know that there is a great scarcity of executive and secretarial help in many Christian organizations (including Campus Crusade). If executives and secretaries are fully dedicated to Christ, they can make a vital contribution to the effectiveness of any Christian ministry. By sharing the ministry with others who have been called to devote their time almost exclusively to evangelism and discipleship, the overall ministry for Christ in such an organization is strengthened greatly. In this way, they can more fully utilize their talents in helping to seek and save the lost.

Faith and Action

One further word of explanation must be given. It is true that God still reveals His will to some men and women in dramatic ways, but this should be considered the exception rather than the rule. God still leads men today as He has through the centuries.

For example, Philip, the deacon, was holding a successful city-wide campaign in Samaria. However, God overruled by a special revelation to give him another assignment which was not consistent with human reason. Philip was led by the Holy Spirit to leave his city-wide ministry to witness to one Ethiopian eunuch. According to tradition, God used the Ethopian eunuch to communicate the message of our living Lord to his entire country.

Living according to the sound mind principle allows for such dramatic leadings of God. But we are not to wait for such revelations before we start moving for Christ. Faith must have an object. A Christian's faith is built upon the authority of God's Word supported by historical fact — and not upon shallow, emotional experience. Consequently, a Christian's trust in God's will as revealed in His Word will result in the decisions which are made by following the sound mind principle.

The confirmation may come in various ways and with respect to many factors, including the personality of the individual involved. Usually, the confirmation is a quiet, peaceful assurance that you are doing what God wants you to do, with the expectancy that God will use you to bear "much fruit."

As any sincere Christian gives himself to a diligent study of the Scriptures and allows a loving, all-wise, sovereign God and Father to control his life, feelings will inevitably follow. Thus, the end result of a life that is lived in obedience to God and His Word is the most joyful, abundant and fruitful life of all.

Expect the Lord Jesus Christ to draw men to Himself through you. As you begin each day, acknowledge the fact that you belong to Him. Thank Him for the fact that He lives within you. Invite Him to walk around in your body. Invite Him to use your mind to think His thoughts, your heart to express His love, your lips to witness for Him. Invite Him to continue seeking and saving souls through you.

Why not begin today by making a list of all the pros and cons of the various ways you can best maximize your life for Christ?

It is my sincere prayer that you may know this exciting, supernatural life-style — that you will find the same day-to-day, moment-by-moment victories that so many others have found by applying the sound mind principle. Above all I pray that you may fully appropriate all that God has given to you as your rightful heritage in Christ in order that you may daily experience God's supernatural will for your life.

CHAPTER TWELVE

The Supernatural Power of Praise

Praise to God releases His supernatural power!

The experience of praising God as an expression of my love and faith has been a tremendously meaningful aspect of my life. There are times when my heart is filled with sorrow. There are times when the burdens of the day are so great that I find myself weighted down — until I am reminded to praise God.

Recently, during a time of financial need for Here's Life, World, I faced the greatest challenge of my entire Christian life. I saw the vast potential of what would happen should God supply this particular need. Millions of people, and ultimately hundreds of millions, could come into Christ's kingdom as a result of these pilot Here's Life cities. But the funds needed seemed far beyond our reach. And yet, as I came to the Lord again and again, I found myself praising and worshiping Him as an act of obedience and faith, in spite of this tremendous pressure.

At the very last hours, before the deadline approached, the miracle happened — God honored our praise, and the funds were supplied. Again and again God has honored my times of praise as an expression of my trust in Him and obedience to His Word. On numerous occasions problems have been solved, funds have been supplied, tears have been turned to joy because of my practice of praise.

Language of Heaven

Praise is the language of heaven. The more we praise God in this life, the more we experience the joys and blessings of heaven. In Revelation we read, "After this I heard the shouting of a vast crowd in heaven, 'Hallelujah! Praise the Lord! Salvation is from our God. Honor and authority belong to Him alone; for His judgments are just and true.' . . . Again and again their voices rang, 'Praise the Lord!' . . . Then the twenty-four Elders and four Living Beings fell down and worshiped God, who was sitting upon the throne, and said, 'Amen! Hallelujah! Praise the Lord!' And out of the throne came a voice that said, 'Praise our God, all of you His servants, small and great, who fear Him.' Then I heard again what sounded like the shouting of a huge crowd, or like the waves of a hundred oceans crashing on the shore, or like the mighty rolling of great thunder, 'Praise the Lord. For the Lord our God, the Almighty, reigns.' "[1]

If we as Christians are going to be prepared to spend all eternity with Christ, we need to learn how to praise Him here on earth. When you find yourself discouraged, when the pressures are greater than you can bear, when your heart is cold and you don't want to praise Him, that is the time to praise the Lord. Praise is as much an expression of the will as it is of the heart, and one who praises God as an expression of the will by faith is soon praising God out of the depths of his innermost being.

If you are saying that the importance of praise is a new concept to you, I can understand. Most of my early years as a Christian were spent in begging and pleading with God, asking for things. But the more I have come to know and love Jesus Christ and the more I have seen His miraculous power at work in my life, the more I am prone to balance my prayer life with praise to Him. I find that more can be accomplished in and through my life for the glory of God through praise than through any other one thing.

Worthy of Praise

I would like to share with you several reasons why I believe praise of God is so important in the life of the believer.

First, our God is truly worthy of praise. He is worthy of praise because of who He is and because of all that He has done for us. The psalmist reminds us, "Praise the Lord! Yes, really praise Him! I will praise Him as long as I live, yes, even with my dying breath."[2]

We praise God for who He is — for His attributes — His love, His sovereignty, His wisdom, His power, His greatness, goodness and compassion, for His faithfulness, His holiness and eternal, unchanging nature.

These and other characteristics of God are described in many passages. Three of my favorites are Isaiah 40, Psalms 139 and Psalms 145-150. There are so many similar passages which help us to realize the greatness of our God. I am increasingly committed to the importance of teaching new and old believers alike the attributes of God, because He is the object of our faith. One cannot really live the life of faith apart from knowing our great and mighty God for who He is. Praise should always begin with emphasis on God and His attributes, and I begin each day praising Him for who He is: my sovereign, righteous, loving, compassionate, all-powerful, never-changing, all-knowing God.

We praise God for His benefits to us. Though too numerous to mention, some of them are expressed in Psalms 103: "He forgives all my sins. He heals me. He ransoms me from hell. He surrounds me with lovingkindness and tender mercies. He fills my life with good things! My youth is renewed like the eagle's!

"He gives justice to all who are treated unfairly. . . . He is merciful and tender toward those who don't deserve it; He is slow to get angry and full of kindness and love. . . . He has not punished us as we deserve for all our sins. . . . He is like a father to us, tender and sympathetic to those who reverence Him. . . . The lovingkindness of the Lord is from everlasting to everlasting, to those who reverence Him; His salvation is to children's children of those who are faithful to His covenant and remember to obey Him!"[3]

No wonder the psalmist concluded this list of great benefits by calling upon all who read this passage, "Let everything everywhere bless [praise] the Lord. And how I bless [praise] Him too!"[4]

Yes, we are to praise God first of all because of who He is, and then we should not take for granted the benefits we enjoy because we belong to Him. How wonderful to know that 2,000 years ago, God in His infinite wisdom and love came down to this little speck of dust called earth, a mere speck in the galaxy of which we are a part, and that galaxy is only a grain of sand in the billions of galaxies which He created. Yet He became one of us in the person of Jesus of Nazareth, both perfect God and perfect man. He was not only the Son of God, but He also was God the Son, the "visible expression of the invisible God."

We should praise Him daily for who He is and for these and many other benefits. How can mere human tongue begin to describe the goodness of God and the wonder of His grace toward us?

Closer to God

Second, praise draws us closer to God. As a result of an extremely busy schedule which takes me from country to country and continent to continent, sometimes my body is weary, my mind is fatigued and my heart is cold — yet as I begin to praise God as an act of the will, reading psalms of praise or entering into songs of worship, my heart begins to warm, and I sense the presence of God. Soon I am praising God out of a full and grateful heart of love for Him. I carry with me a small cassette player and several cassettes of praise music which I usually play each morning and evening. I begin and end each day praising Him. Also, it is a source of encouragement to be reminded when I am weary that the Lord Jesus was also weary in His ministry while here on earth — yet He went far beyond being weary — He died and shed His blood for us. We cannot do too much for Him.

Third, all who praise God are blessed. In Isaiah we read, "The Lord will show the nations of the world His justice; all will praise Him. His righteousness shall be like a budding tree, or like a garden in early spring, full of young plants springing up everywhere."[5]

The psalmist wrote, "Let all the joys of the godly well up in praise to the Lord, for it is right to praise Him. Play joyous melodies of praise upon the lyre and on the harp. Compose new songs of praise to Him, accompanied skillfully on the harp; sing joyfully. For all God's words are right, and everything He does is worthy of our trust."[6] Something happens to the man who praises God. His life is blessed and enriched, and he is strengthened.

Fourth, praise is contagious. God's Word admonishes us, "Let each generation tell its children what glorious things He does."[7] Similar words are found in Psalms 79:13, "Then we Your people, the sheep of Your pasture, will thank You forever and forever, praising Your greatness from generation to generation."

As you can see, praise is intended to be spread. And God, our heavenly Father, has ordained that we begin spreading the joy of praise in our own homes. I have never prayed that our sons, Zachary and Bradley, would become wealthy, famous, brilliant or scholarly. But I pray daily that they will know God for who He is and that He will be real in their experience. I pray that my sons will trust and obey our Lord Jesus Christ and live holy lives that will honor Him. I pray for them as I pray for myself and for my beloved wife, Vonette, for the Campus Crusade staff and their families and for our support team and their families, that there will be a quality of life about us, a supernatural life-style of praise, thanksgiving and love, that will cause others to want to know our wonderful Lord and to follow Him who alone is worthy of our praise.

A Praising Church

I have spoken in hundreds of different churches of all denominations. Some churches exalt Christ and preach His Word. They are filled with praise and with love for God and one another. For the most part, such churches are growing steadily and have no serious problems, financial or otherwise. Because they consist of men and women who have discovered the power of praise, theirs is a vital, attractive faith.

On the other hand, I have been in churches which are cold and unfriendly. There the members gather routinely to worship the historical Christ and go away unchanged — just as carnal and critical and unbelieving as when they arrived. No praise, no worship; nothing to attract either unbelievers or believers looking for a vital faith and fellowship.

I would encourage all pastors and all church members to make sure their various services are filled with praise and worship — from the opening hymn, through the reading of Scripture, the prayers, the sermon, the anthem, to the closing hymn. Make sure your sanctuary reflects the presence of God so that those who come to worship the living Christ will be met with a warm welcome and experience the joy of praising God.

Some time ago I worshiped in a strange church where I did not expect to meet anyone I knew. I was surprised to be received so warmly. I thought at first such a reception might be because I was recognized, but when I looked around, I saw that everyone was being greeted in the same friendly manner.

I made it a point to ask one of the greeters what made the church so warm and friendly. He explained that a man who was no longer living had *taught* them how to be outgoing for the Lord. He had influenced the previous generation of the church with a spirit that had been passed on to the present generation. He taught them that Christians should go out of their way to be warm and loving as representatives of our Lord. That man's witness of praise to the living God had done as much to enhance the worship and fellowship of that particular church as anything else could possibly have done. You, too, can be such a spark to help make fellowship with God and with one another come alive in your church.

Sixth, Satan's power is broken when we praise God. I always enjoy reading II Chronicles 20 with regard to this point. It is a dramatic story of how God honored Jehoshaphat's praise to Him by giving victory over the enemy.

Praise and Victory

You may recall that Jehoshaphat received word that the combined armies of Ammon, Moab and Mount Seir had declared war on him and the people of Judah and Jerusalem. When the news reached him that this vast host was marching against him, he was badly shaken and determined to beg for help from the Lord.

So he announced that all the people of Judah should go without food for a time and be penitent before God. From across the nation the people of Judah came to Jerusalem to plead unitedly with God, and Jehoshaphat stood among them as they gathered before the temple and prayed, "O our God, won't You stop them? We have no way to protect ourselves against this mighty army. We don't know what to do, but we are looking to You."[8]

God responded by assuring them of victory and commanded them to take the offensive.

The next morning when the army of Judah was making preparations to march against the enemy, Jehoshaphat called them to attention and said, "Listen to me, O people of Judah and Jerusalem. . . . Believe in the Lord your God, and you shall have success!"[9]

God instructed Jehoshaphat "that there should be a choir leading the march, clothed in sanctified garments and singing the song 'His Loving Kindness Is Forever' as they walked along praising and thanking the Lord! And at the moment they began to sing and to praise, the Lord caused the armies of Ammon, Moab, and Mount Seir to begin fighting among themselves." We are told that their destruction of each other was so complete that all the people of Judah had to do was load up the spoil from the battle and return to Jerusalem. But as they were returning, we are told that "they gathered in the Valley of Blessing . . . and how they praised the Lord!"[10]

There is tremendous power in praise. Again and again, when attacks have been made against various movements of God by those who are not of the Lord's kingdom, I have found that praise of God releases His power in behalf of His people.

For example, we were at the University of California in Berkeley in 1966, the very week that the president of the university was fired by the Board of Regents. The campuses throughout California erupted in violence.

On the Berkeley campus, however, about 600 Campus Crusade staff and students were there to present the claims of Jesus Christ to over 27,000 students. During the week, through some 80 meetings in dormitories, in fraternity and sorority houses and international groups, in athletic banquets and faculty breakfasts and luncheons, in personal appointments and finally at a great meeting of some 8,000 gathered in the Greek Theater, the campus was truly saturated with the gospel.

A "Radical" Difference

When the camera crews from the local television stations rushed out to film the violence which had been predicted and which was actually happening all over the state — the reporters were amazed to discover that the Berkeley campus, the fountainhead of the radical student revolution, was amazingly quiet. All over the campus there was music and singing and sharing about the love of God.

Light is more powerful than darkness. Whenever we exalt the Son of God, who is the light of the world, darkness — Satan's kingdom — flees. In times of attack from the enemy, praise God and see the enemy flee from you.

Seventh, praise is a witness to carnal Christians and non-Christians. Centuries ago, St. Augustine proclaimed: "Thou hast made us for Thyself, O God, and our hearts are restless until they find their rest in Thee."[11]

It has been my experience that around the world in most countries and cultures you will find a high percentage of the masses of people looking for God — but most of them do not know how to find Him.

Certainly they are drawn to God when they see an attractive, contagious witness in the lives of those who profess to be His followers.

There is a slogan concerning a particular automobile: "Ask the man who owns one." So it is with our Christian faith. If we expect others to be drawn to Jesus Christ, there must be a quality of life in us that is attractive to them.

Oh, how much defeated Christians need the example of joyful Christian lives. And the more radiant and joyful Christians are, the more non-Christians will want what they have. There is such great loneliness in the world, so much heartache, so much sorrow, and as Christians walk in the light and reflect the light in their countenances and conduct, many will want to follow the one whom they serve. When you look in the mirror, do you see a joyful, happy face or a long, sober face? Out of the heart are the issues of life, and when praise is most on our hearts, praise will be most on our lips and joy in our countenances.

I have found that the most vocal and effective voices against faith in Christ and His church are of those who were reared in the church — often in churches which were rigid and dogmatic about their beliefs to the extreme. Frequently their fathers and mothers professed to believe in Christ and attended church where the members communicated that they were the only "true Christianity." So these young people grew up in an atmosphere filled with criticism and suspicion. Hence, when the children grew to adulthood, they rejected the faith of their parents and the teachings of the church to which they had been exposed.

Tragic Consequences

Today, some of the leading people in government, education and the media trace their spiritual heritage to fathers who were ministers or to family members who professed to be Christians but who did not live a life of victory and joy. For example, a well-known news commentator recently did an hour-long television special ridiculing "born-again" Christianity. The commentator is an ordained minister who had "walked the sawdust trail and had an emotional experience" in his youth.

However, he had been turned away from the church because of the hypocrisy to which he had been exposed. Now, he finds it difficult to believe that there is any validity to evangelical Christianity. Thus, it is all the more important that those of us who truly believe in the Lord Jesus Christ demonstrate our faith through living lives of joy and victory. In so doing, we shall influence the cold, carnal and unbelieving world.

Eighth, praise opens our hearts and minds to hear God. Nothing is more helpful to me in my prayer life than to spend much of my time in praise and listening to God. For as I praise God, my thoughts are no longer focused on myself. As I concentrate on Him, He has greater opportunity to speak to me, telling me what He wants me to do.

Prayer and Praise

Yes, God actually talks to us — if we are willing to listen. Indeed, one of the best ways to prepare our spiritual ears to hear His instructions is to praise Him. Today, most of my prayer life is spent praising God and giving Him thanks for who He is and for all the benefits and blessings which I enjoy because I belong to Him.

I believe the Scriptures when they say, "You do not have because you do not ask." However, it is as we praise God and give thanks to Him that our minds are opened so that we know best how to pray and what to pray for, for He makes intercession for us in "groanings that cannot be uttered."[19]

Ninth, praise is a form of sacrifice. Hebrews 13:15 says, "Through Him then, let us continually offer up a sacrifice of praise to God, that is, the fruit of lips that give thanks to His name."

With Jesus' help, we are able continually to offer our sacrifice of praise to God by telling others of the glory of His name. In doing so, we soon discover that sacrifice — particularly the sacrifice of praise — becomes an increasingly joyous thing. Also, we find that telling others about God — sharing the joy of praise — creates great blessing in our lives as well as in those with whom we share.

Tenth, praise makes for a more joyful life. You may say, "I don't feel like praising God. I don't have anything to praise Him for." Actually, praise is as much an expression of the will as it is of the heart. We are the ones who determine whether or not we want to praise God.

As I have suggested, there are times when my heart is less filled with praise than others. My mind may be fatigued from travel or I may be facing difficult problems and decisions. But as I open the Scriptures to the Psalms and other portions of God's Word which call me to praise, my heart is soon singing and making melody to the Lord. In such instances, I have chosen to praise God as an act of my will. And, as a result, I come genuinely to praise Him through His enabling power.

Courage and Hope

The psalmist says, "Take courage, my soul! Do you remember those times . . . when you led a great procession to the Temple on festival days, singing with joy, praising the Lord? Why then be downcast? Why be discouraged and sad? Hope in God! I shall yet praise Him again. Yes, I shall again praise Him for His help."[14]

There may be times when you experience defeat and depression. But like the psalmist, you can choose to rejoice in the Lord, and as you do so as an act of your will, your heart — your emotions — will begin to rejoice. In fact, God's Word commands us to "rejoice in the Lord always; again I will say, rejoice!"

Eleventh, praise enhances human relationships. The individual whose life is filled with praise to God is pleasant to be with. He whose heart is filled with praise becomes more and more like Christ and as a result is more loving, forgiving, considerate, compassionate and kind.

Therefore, the one who truly praises God is the best kind of friend you can find. When husbands and wives praise God together, the result is like a beautiful symphony. When families praise God, it is a joy to God and for all to behold. Surely there is no example on earth more convincing of the validity of the Christian faith and the reality of the living God than that family which truly honors the Lord Jesus Christ and fills the days with praise to God.

Twelfth, praise is a supernatural expression of faith. I encourage you to make a list of everything for which you can praise God. Read appropriate psalms for ideas, and then take a sheet of paper and begin to list the attributes of God and all the benefits and blessings which you receive from Him.

Growing in Praise

Praise God for who He is. Praise Him that He loves you. Praise Him for having forgiven your sins. Praise Him that through Christ's death and resurrection you have eternal life. Praise Him that He orders your daily steps. Praise Him for loved ones, for friends, for good health, for daily provisions. Praise Him for the privilege of living and even of suffering, if need be, for Him.

You will grow in your praise of God through songs, through the reading of psalms of praise, and through your discipline of beginning and ending each day by meditating on His attributes. In time, praise will become an unconscious act. It will be something you greatly desire to do, so much so that your day will not be complete without it.

Remember, at the heart of the joyful, successful, radiant, attractive, fruitful, Spirit-filled life is a life of praise to God. No Christian can begin to approach spiritual maturity whose life is not characterized by praise.

I have known this truth for many years and have practiced it throughout that time. But the more I practice it, the more I feel like a child who is just learning how really to praise God.

I commend to you a supernatural life of praise.

CHAPTER THIRTEEN

The Supernatural Power of Thanksgiving

The telephone rang. I answered it, and heard the voice of one of my dear friends and co-laborers reporting that his young son had just died unexpectedly. Understandably, both of us were deeply moved. My friend and his wife had lost their beloved son, but already they were praising and thanking God, even through their tears and with broken hearts . . .

Another dear friend and staff member instructed the pastor and choir that the memorial service for his young wife who had been suddenly killed in a tragic automobile accident should be filled with praise and worship to God. He gives radiant testimony of our Lord's faithfulness: "Peace I leave with you";[1] "Come to Me, all who are weary and heavy laden, and I will give you rest."[2]

A Christian couple are thanking and praising God for the doctor's diagnosis of the wife's inoperable cancer . . .

Jim and Betty, beloved friends and associate staff, were inseparable. They were attending staff training a few weeks ago. Suddenly and unexpectedly, during a meeting, Jim had a massive heart attack and went to be with the Lord instantly. As an act of obedience Betty began to praise and give thanks to God through her tears . . .

A businessman shared how he had lost everything he had. He had once been wealthy, successful and influential with a palatial home, several automobiles and millions of dollars. He had enjoyed the "good life," and now it was all gone. And yet he was saying, "Thank You, Lord."

How can men and women who are experiencing adversity, heartache and sorrow say "Thank You" to God? It seems so incongruous and so contrary to the ways of the world, where the norm is to react to adversity with negative attitudes of hate and fear and resentment.

A Way of Life

Yet thanksgiving is a way of life for those who have discovered how to live a supernatural life by believing God for the impossible.

Obviously, these and others about whom I could speak did not necessarily *feel* thankful. But something wonderful had happened in their lives. Something supernatural had taken place when they received Christ, the gift of God's love, as their Lord and Savior. They no longer thought and acted like non-believers, but had become spiritual creatures. Now they were living a supernatural kind of life in their desire to be obedient to our Lord. As we are admonished to do in I Thessalonians, they learned, "In everything give thanks; for this is God's will for you in Christ Jesus."[3]

A thankful attitude is a characteristic of the Spirit-filled life. Immediately following God's command for His children to be "filled with the Holy Spirit," as recorded in Ephesians 5:18, we are further instructed in the following verses, "Talk with each other much about the Lord, quoting psalms and hymns and singing sacred songs, making music in your hearts to the Lord. *Always give thanks for everything to our God and Father in the name of our Lord Jesus Christ*"[4] [italics mine].

Thankful for Everything?

"Always give thanks for everything?" my friend Jim responded with impatience which bordered on anger. "How can I give thanks to God when my wife is dying of cancer? I would be a fool, and besides, I don't feel thankful. My heart is breaking. I can't stand to see her suffer any more."

Although Jim was a Christian, he had not yet learned how to appropriate the supernatural resources of God by faith. He had not heard that the Holy Spirit produces the supernatural, spiritual fruit of love, joy, peace, patience, kindness, goodness, faithfulness, gentleness and self-control. He did not know that the Holy Spirit is ready and eager to lift his load, fill his heart with peace and enable him to demonstrate a thankful attitude, even in times of heartache, sorrow and disappointment.

About the same time I met with Jim a telephone call came from a beloved friend and fellow staff member, Bob. "I am calling to ask for your prayers," he said. "Alice [his wife] has an inoperable brain tumor, but we are trusting the Lord for a miracle. We are both thanking God," he continued, "for we know He makes no mistakes, and we are ready for whatever happens."

Spirit-filled Thanksgiving

What a contrast in attitudes! Jim was fearful, anxious and bitter. "Why does this have to happen to us?" he complained. "How could a loving God allow anyone, especially a Christian, to suffer such pain and agony?"

Bob and Alice, on the other hand, were at peace, trusting God and giving thanks.

What was the difference? Bob and Alice were controlled by the Holy Spirit and were responding as Spirit-filled persons are equipped to respond — according to God's Word.

The days, weeks, months and eventually more than a year passed as Alice's health grew continually worse. All the while she and Bob were thanking God. Though there was no miraculous healing of Alice's sick body, God performed a greater miracle as He provided the supernatural resources which enabled Bob and Alice to give powerful testimony of God's love and grace.

Shortly before she went to be with our Lord, I visited her, Bob and the children in the hospital. As I entered her room she was smiling. Someone asked, "Alice, why are you smiling?" She replied, "Oh, the Lord is so good to me." Only a Spirit-filled person can experience such joy and peace and demonstrate such a thankful attitude.

It is God's command to "always give thanks for everything." Along with each command which God makes there is a promise, either spoken or implied. In essence, He says, "If you trust and obey Me, I will enable you by the power of My Spirit to do what I have commanded you to do."

Thanking by Faith

The Word of God constantly reminds us that we are to live by faith: "Without faith it is impossible to please God." When we respond to God with a spirit of thanksgiving — even in times of difficulty — we are demonstrating our faith.

Many years ago there was an occasion when my world was crumbling. All that I had worked and planned for in the ministry of Campus Crusade was hanging by a slender thread which was about to break. Because of a series of unforeseen circumstances, we were facing a financial crisis which could bankrupt the movement and result in the loss of our beautiful facilities at Arrowhead Springs, Calif., acquired just three years before. Already thousands of students and laymen from all over the world were receiving training which would influence millions of lives for Christ. Now we were in danger of losing it all.

God's Power Released

When the word came to me that everything we had planned and prayed for was in jeopardy and almost certain to be lost, I fell to my knees and began to give thanks to the Lord. Why? Because many years before I had discovered that thanksgiving demonstrates faith, and faith pleases God. When we demonstrate faith through thanksgiving, as an expression of obedience and gratitude to God, He releases His great power in our behalf so that we can serve Him better.

God fights the battles for those who trust and obey Him. By acknowledging our faith in Him, even though circumstances would suggest that there is no hope, He miraculously intervenes. Tragedy turns to triumph, discord to harmony, and defeat to victory.

And so, as I was praising and thanking God, His supernatural peace flooded my heart, and I began to sense that God was going to work a special kind of miracle in my life and in the ministry of Campus Crusade. I received the assurance that the miracle for which we had earlier prayed — and was now being denied us — would be far overshadowed by the second miracle which God would work.

In a matter of a few days, totally apart from any of my own abilities to solve the problem, God brought the right people into the right circumstances and performed that second — and greater — miracle! My faith did a quantum leap as God miraculously provided the necessary finances to save Arrowhead Springs for the ministry.

God Is Faithful

As I was writing this chapter, I was sitting in the waiting room at Loma Linda Hospital. My beloved wife, Vonette, had been in major surgery for four hours. Three weeks before, her doctor had informed her that she had a large growth which could be malignant.

The doctor had wanted to operate at once but had agreed to wait until I returned from a tour of several Latin American countries where we were launching Here's Life. When Vonette called me in Brazil, I suggested that I return home at once, but she insisted that I not interrupt the meetings which could ultimately result in training hundreds of thousands of Christians who would help to reach millions for our Lord.

We prayed together over the telephone, praising God for the faithfulness He had shown to us in the past. We also thanked Him for the situation, as an act of obedience to His Word. As we praised and thanked the Lord, His supernatural peace flooded our hearts. During the following weeks we continued to praise and thank Him as we both continued to speak and witness for Him in many meetings, recognizing that we are His servants, and the Master is responsible for the welfare of His servants.

After the surgery the doctors assured us that the operation was a success and that there was no malignancy. We continue to thank and praise the Lord for His goodness to us.

In Romans 8:28, we read one of God's great promises to us: "All things work together for good to them that love God, to them who are the called according to His purpose" (KJV). Do you believe this promise of God? If you do, then you can logically acknowledge the reasonableness of God's command to always give thanks.

Command and Promise

Like Jim, the young friend I mentioned earlier, you may say that only a fool would give thanks to God in times of tragedy and despair. But such is not the case if "all things work together for good to those who love God." If God has commanded us to give thanks, there is a reason for it. And as He has promised to work all things for good "to those who love Him," you can trust Him and His command and His promise.

There are three ways in particular in which our lives are enriched when we, in every way and under all circumstances, respond with thanksgiving. According to Scripture, when we

are thankful in all circumstances, God supernaturally releases *peace, joy* and *provision* for our daily needs.

In Colossians 3:15 we read, "Let the peace of heart which
comes from Christ be always present in your hearts and lives,
for this is your responsibility and privilege as members of His
body. And always be thankful" (Living). Note the context! God
promises the "peace of Christ" when we are thankful, and that
peace comes as both our *privilege* and our *responsibility*.

What a Privilege!

It is our privilege because God loves us and has chosen us
to be His own. We cannot manufacture the peace of Christ
through emotions or feelings. The peace of Christ is a supernatural peace which we can experience only as He lives His
supernatural, resurrection life in and through us. And in
order to experience the spiritual privilege of that peace, we
must exercise a spiritual responsibility: as an act of our will,
as an act of obedience, we must be thankful.

What is the nature of the supernatural peace which the
Bible calls "the peace of Christ"? In Philippians 4:6,7, Paul
gives us a clear answer: "Don't worry about anything; instead,
pray about everything; tell God your needs and don't forget to
thank Him for His answers. If you do this you will experience
God's peace, which is far more wonderful than the human
mind can understand. His peace will keep your thoughts and
your hearts quiet and at rest as you trust in Christ Jesus"
(Living). Both the Revised Standard and the King James
versions describe the peace as being that which "passes all
understanding."

Peace and Joy

Note again the context. Being thankful is an integral part
of our communication with God. We are to pray and ask God to
provide for our needs. But equally important, we are to "thank
Him for His answers." We are expected to be obedient in
thanking God in response to hearing our prayers. If we are
thus obedient, God promises to grant us the supernatural
peace which the human mind cannot understand (because we
cannot, on our own, create that kind of peace). And this peace
will keep our thoughts and hearts "quiet and at rest" as we —
in thankfulness — "trust in Christ Jesus."

Psalms 147:7 encourages us to "sing to the Lord with thanksgiving." Isaiah 51:3 records God's promise that there is "joy and gladness" in the thankful "voice of song." You might say from these scriptural illustrations that thanksgiving is a spiritual way of singing. As we sing with a thankful heart, we receive the joy of the Lord in return.

In Hebrews 13:15, thanksgiving is described as "the fruit of our lips." Here is another example of the dual nature of thanksgiving: it is both a privilege and a responsibility. As an act of the will by faith we offer our sacrifice of praise. With Jesus' help we will continually offer our sacrifice of praise to God by telling others of the glory of His name.

Cast All Your Cares

Recently, the editors of a Christian publication came to Arrowhead Springs to interview me. Our discussion turned to the subject of "problems" in the Christian life, and they questioned me concerning the way in which I handle difficult circumstances which are potential sources of anxiety and frustration.

I explained that many years ago I learned to obey God's command to be thankful in all things. And since I am assured from God's Word that God loves me, I would be very foolish indeed to worry about my problems, cares and tribulations even for a few moments. I cast them upon the Lord as soon as they are brought to my attention.

For example, I can list at least 25 major problems that I have given to the Lord today — some of which would crush me and destroy my effectiveness if I tried to carry them myself. And I can recall one recent week in which my wife, mother-in-law, sister and niece were in the hospital; a brother was scheduled for surgery; and some of my associates had lost loved ones. Several other major personal problems, as well as the need to raise several million dollars to finance strategic Here's Life cities overseas, were constantly before me.

There were more problems than usual that week, but I chose to obey the Lord's command to give them to Him. "Let Him have all your worries and cares, for He is always thinking about you and watching everything that concerns you."[5] In so doing I always find His promise to be true; His yoke *is* easy and His burden *is* light.[6]

God's Word assures us that problems and trials are always a blessing for the trusting, obedient Christian. It even encourages us to be *happy* when our lives are full of difficulties and temptations because it will produce a supernatural faith. "Dear brothers, is your life full of difficulties and temptations? Then be happy, for when the way is rough, your patience has a chance to grow. So let it grow, and don't try to squirm out of your problems. For when your patience is finally in full bloom, then you will be ready for anything, strong in character, full and complete."[7]

Declaration of Independence

Remember, even as God gave the Law to Moses on two tablets, your spiritual "declaration of independence" has been divinely etched in two passages in Scripture:

Romans 8:28 — "And we know that all that happens to us is working for our good if we love God and are fitting into His plans" (Living).

I Thessalonians 5:18 — "No matter what happens, always be thankful, for this is God's will for you who belong to Christ Jesus" (Living).

Declare your freedom from the burdens and despair of this world by trusting the Holy Spirit to enable you to be thankful in all circumstances, and by never forgetting to thank God for answered prayer. God has ordained that you experience His peace, His joy and a full and abundant life in a way that the "human mind cannot comprehend." And He has ordained that such a supernatural experience be the fruit of thankful hearts.

Spirit-controlled Security

Picture in your mind's eye a bird sitting on the limb of a tree, sheltered in the cleft of a rock from a terrible storm raging all around it. Sensing its security, the bird sings sweetly as the thunder roars, the lightning flashes, and the wind blows with hurricane strength. So it is with a Spirit-controlled Christian who has learned the secret of praising and thanking God in all things as an expression of faith and obedience. The storms of life gather, the trials, temptations and testings descend like a plague — yet God's grace is so abundant, His peace and joy so supernatural that a Christian can indeed rejoice and give thanks in all things.

May I suggest that you pause right now with pen and paper and make a list of all the things for which you should thank God, both good and bad. Thank Him for every disappointment, heartache, sorrow and personal problem as well as for all of the good things which you enjoy.

Ask God to seal upon your heart the assurance that as you thank Him *in all circumstances* He will indeed work all things for good as you grow more and more to trust and obey Him. Ask Him to enable you to give thanks as an act of the will, even when you do not feel like it. Trust Him to release His supernatural power into your life as you demonstrate a truly thankful spirit.

CHAPTER FOURTEEN

The Supernatural Blessings of Discipleship

Jesus was constantly involved in ministering to multitudes of people, but He also spent much time discipling those closest to Him, especially the twelve. He considered discipling so important that He included it in His command to help fulfill the Great Commission: "Teach these new disciples to obey all the commands I have given you."[1]

The apostle Paul took seriously our Lord's command. To the Colossians he wrote, "So everywhere we go we talk about Christ to all who will listen, warning them and teaching them as well as we know how. We want to be able to present each one to God, perfect because of what Christ has done for each of them."[2] And in his second letter to Timothy, Paul said, "For you must teach others those things you and many others have heard me speak about. Teach these great truths to trustworthy men who will, in turn, pass them on to others."[3]

Evangelism, the Beginning

You will observe that the apostle Paul placed a strong emphasis on evangelism, but he did not stop there. He recognized the importance of bringing new converts to spiritual maturity so that they, in turn, would teach the things they had learned to still others. Thus, we can see that the principles of evangelism, discipleship and spiritual multiplication were intertwined in everything Paul did, just as they were in the life of our Lord.

This is our example. We are to be involved constantly in sharing our faith in Christ. In introducing men and women to Christ, however, we should realize that successful witnessing is simply taking the initiative to share Christ in the power of the Holy Spirit, leaving the results to God. We are to be involved in sharing our faith as a way of life. But we are not to be under pressure to "get decisions." Nor are we to put others under such pressure.

Simply Follow Jesus

It is our responsibility simply to follow Jesus; it is His responsibility to make us "fishers of men."[4] We do not make converts — that is the work of the Holy Spirit. But, if we are obedient to Christ, we will share the good news at every opportunity; and in so doing, we will do everything within our power to help these new converts grow and mature in Christ.

We are all to be witnesses,[5] though not every Christian has the spiritual gift of evangelism. Many Christians who leave evangelism to those with the "gift" miss much of the joy and exciting adventure of the Christian life because of their disobedience or misunderstanding of their responsibility to witness.

Other Christians give up regular witnessing because they do not see tangible results in terms of decisions for Christ when they witness. But God promises to bless those who obey Him. Not to share our faith regularly is to disobey God and to miss His blessings.

Leave Results to God

Again, it is not our responsibility to make converts. That is God's responsibility. It is our responsibility to be faithful witnesses and to leave the results to Him.

Perhaps the most exciting result of obeying our Lord's command to "teach new disciples" is that God has ordained a number of blessings for us, including the fact that the Lord Himself is pleased when we "go and make disciples."

One such special blessing can be seen in the promise which Jesus gives in John 14:21, "He who has My commandments and keeps them, he it is who loves Me; and he who loves Me shall be loved by My Father, and I will love him, and will disclose Myself to him."[6]

There is something exciting and wonderfully unique about seeing one whom you have discipled grow and mature, and lead others to Christ and disciple them. Such an experience often brings even more excitement than is derived from your own, personal ministry.

For example, I take special delight and pleasure whenever our sons, Zachary or Bradley, do something special for the Lord — much more than if I were doing it personally.

In a similar vein, the spiritual blessings that accrue through the life of one whom you are discipling are even more meaningful than when you are personally involved.

Spiritual Multiplication

Furthermore, by investing your life in helping others to grow in the Lord, you will in turn be helping still others to experience the abundant life which only true disciples of the Lord Jesus Christ experience. In effect, you will be able to multiply yourself spiritually.

Some years ago, I experienced this blessing when a member of our staff handed me a copy of *Sports Illustrated.* The picture on the cover was the recent choice for the Heisman Trophy, which, as you probably know, means that the young man had been selected as the year's No. 1 collegiate football player.

As the staff member handed the magazine to me, he said, "I would like to introduce you to your great grandson."

"What do you mean?" I asked.

"Well," he said, "you led Jim to Christ, Jim led me to Christ, and I led Steve [the Heisman winner] to Christ." Naturally, I rejoiced!

And so it is, wherever I go around the world, I meet men and women who have received Christ through someone who has been directly or indirectly related to my own personal ministry of evangelism and discipleship.

No Generation Gap

Only yesterday a young Christian leader took me to an appointment. "You are my spiritual grandfather," he said. "You led Bob to Christ, and he introduced me to Christ." The next day I had lunch with one of the leading citizens of a large city whom my spiritual "grandson" had introduced to Christ, making this businessman my spiritual "great-grandson."

And, as is the case with true spiritual multiplication, you will invariably find that your example serves in turn to encourage other Christians to build disciples in obedience to our Lord's command — as the illustration about our staff member and his Heisman-Trophy-winning friend demonstrates.

By helping to build disciples, you will experience the supernatural blessing which comes from helping to accelerate the fulfillment of the Great Commission.

Often I think about the dilemma which I faced after the first year of my ministry, trying to determine whether I should concentrate my efforts on evangelism alone or on evangelism *and* discipleship. To this day I praise God for the decision He led me to make, to combine the two emphases.

For example, if, hypothetically, I had led 1,000 people to Christ every day for the last 28 years, there would have been 365,000 people receiving Christ per year, or a total of approximately 10 million new Christians. Yet, by concentrating on building disciples with a view toward evangelism and the fulfillment of the Great Commission, Campus Crusade, with a present staff of approximately 9,000 serving Christ in more than 100 countries, has had the opportunity to train well over one million people in the basic concepts of how to live the abundant, spiritual life and how to share their faith more effectively with others.

Results Unlimited

There is, of course, no possible way to know how many have received Christ as a result of the efforts of our staff and those whom we have trained, but I am sure the number would far exceed the 10 million that theoretically I might have been able to reach for Christ had I been concentrating on evangelism alone and had led 1,000 people to Christ every day for the past 28 years.

Last week I met with our staff and students at Penn State University, where there are 450 students involved in discipleship training. Some of our staff and students introduced me to five and six generations of disciples on the campus. During the past five years literally hundreds have gone into some form of Christian ministry from that campus, through the influence of the trained disciplers — staff and students.

Some years ago I was introduced to a group of medical doctors and students who had been influenced and discipled for Christ through our training center in Manila, Philippines. The first gentleman, a young doctor, gave a brief testimony of how our training center director at that time had introduced him to Christ and discipled him.

Disciple After Disciple

Then he introduced one of those whom he had led to Christ and discipled. This young doctor gave his testimony and introduced one of the medical students whom he had introduced to Christ and discipled. This procedure was followed for six generations, as disciple after disciple stood to give his testimony and introduce one of his disciples. The last medical student was a radiant two-week-old Christian.

To God be the glory! He alone is worthy of our adoration, worship and praise. The very thought of how He has so richly blessed my life and the ministry of Campus Crusade overwhelms me with gratitude and a deep sense of reverence and awe. That is why I feel so strongly impressed to share with each Christian I meet that God greatly blesses those who disciple others in the name of the Lord Jesus Christ.

Of Equal Importance

Evangelism and discipleship are equally important and vital for healthy Christian growth. We cannot separate the two. The more we evangelize, the greater will be the number of those who need to be discipled; and the more we seek to disciple others, the more there will be who will become Christians through their witness; and the more Christians there are, the more opportunities we will have to build additional disciples.

This principle is much like the one which governs the jet engine: the greater the speed, the greater the intake of air; and the greater the intake of air, the greater the thrust; and the greater the thrust, the greater the speed . . . and so on.

It is a law of God: keep on sowing, keep on reaping, keep on evangelizing and keep on discipling.

You may ask, if we are not only to evangelize but also to disciple others, how do we go about it? What goes into bringing a new Christian to maturity in his faith?

Time and space will not allow for lengthy details, but let me list some of the important lessons I have learned about building "committed" disciples.

Leading by Example

First of all, we lead by example. We cannot expect others to become disciples unless we are disciples. We cannot expect

others to become disciplers unless we are disciplers. Like
begets like; we produce after our kind.

I think we are examples in three different ways. We are
examples first by the holy lives we live, by our total commitment to Christ, by the excitement, joy and enthusiasm of our
Spirit-controlled life-style. Second, we are examples by the
fruitfulness of our personal witness for Christ. Third, we are
examples by the priority we give to building disciples.

Those who have influenced me most have been men and
women of God, men and women who have truly known what it
means to be a disciple. In fact, five people come to mind.

Major Influences

My beloved mother, who is now 89, dedicated me to Christ
before I was born and lived an exemplary life before me. Even
during my years of agnosticism, she prayed for me daily. To
this day I have never seen her do an un-Christian act or heard
her say an un-Christian word.

My wife, Vonette, with whom I have had the privilege of
serving our Lord for more than 30 exciting, adventuresome
years, continues to be a daily witness to me.

Dr. Louis Evans, Sr., who was pastor of the First Presbyterian Church of Hollywood when I received Christ, also had a
great influence on my life, as well as Dr. Henrietta Mears, for
many years the well-known director of Christian Education
at the same church. Andrew Murray, a Scottish missionary in
South Africa who lived many years ago, has, through his
writings, influenced me greatly.

A second lesson I've learned is that we build disciples by
praying for them. The Lord Jesus Christ prayed for His disciples and for all who would ultimately believe, including us.
The apostle Paul also prayed for all whom the Lord had placed
in his charge. For example, in Ephesians he writes, "I pray for
you constantly, asking God, the glorious Father of our Lord
Jesus Christ, to give you wisdom to see clearly and really
understand who Christ is and all that He has done for you. I
pray that your hearts will be flooded with light so that you can
see something of the future He has called you to share."[7]

God has entrusted incredible privilege and power to His
children through prayer. At least twice daily I pray for our
staff and their families, as well as for all those who support

this ministry and their families. I claim for them God's super-natural resources that they will grow and mature and become men and women of God, that Christ will be more and more at home in their hearts and that they will be fruitful in their walk with Him.

Prayer for World-changers

I pray that we as a movement will contribute to a super-natural life-style that will help to touch the 20th-century world as the first-century Christians were used of God to influence their generation.

Therefore, when I claim the resources of God for those who are entrusted to my care and for whom the Spirit impresses me to pray, I can know with assurance that He hears me. For we have His promise in I John 5:14,15 that if we ask anything according to God's will He hears us, and if He hears us, He answers us.

Teaching Truths

A third way to build committed disciples is through the teaching of truths necessary to spiritual growth. This involves a number of things:

a. Encourage your disciples to make Christ the Lord of their lives, according to Romans 12:1,2; Galatians 2:20; and other similar passages. Teach them by being an example, by instructing them in God's Word, and by introducing them to other godly men and women. Help them to see the difference between the life-style of the carnal believer and the life-style of those who have made Christ their Lord.

b. Teach them how to walk in the control and power of the Holy Spirit. To emphasize discipleship without a proper understanding of the personal ministry of the Holy Spirit leads to frustration, legalism and all kinds of spiritual problems.

The most liberating truth you can teach your new disciples is the concept of spiritual breathing: how to exhale spiritually by confessing sin, and how to inhale spiritually by appropriating the fullness of God's Spirit by faith as a way of life. There is no truth that is more important than this one.

c. Teach the one whom you are seeking to disciple the importance of God's Word. The Bible is God's holy, inspired word to man. In II Timothy 3:16,17 we read, "The whole Bible was given to us by inspiration from God and is useful to teach us what is true and to make us realize what is wrong in our lives; it straightens us out and helps us do what is right. It is God's way of making us well prepared at every point, fully equipped to do good to everyone."

By example and instruction help your disciples to understand the importance of reading the Word of God regularly, of studying it, memorizing it and meditating upon its truths daily. It is impossible to become a mature disciple without an understanding of God's Word. Help them to realize that there is not a single spiritual problem that they will ever encounter that does not find an answer in the inspired Scriptures. The Holy Spirit confirms in the heart of every true believer the validity and authenticity of the Word which He inspired holy men to record centuries ago.

Let Him Watch

d. Teach your disciple how to witness by letting him watch you. It is not enough to explain all the methods, techniques and strategies; it is not enough to memorize materials. Just as one learns to pray by praying, so one learns to witness by witnessing. It is also helpful if you can teach your disciple how to give his testimony personally to individuals and to groups, both small and large.

For example, we encourage our staff and those whom we train to condense their testimonies into approximately three minutes in length. We encourage them to include what their lives were like before they became Christians, the events that led up to their becoming Christians, how they became Christians, and significant changes which have taken place in their lives since they received Christ.

Also, encourage your disciples to take special courses in public speaking and journalism, so that they might learn how to communicate their faith through the written and spoken word more effectively.

e. Teach your disciples the importance of Christian fellowship, especially through the local church. Approximately 25 years ago, when I first wrote the booklet, "Have You Heard of the Four Spiritual Laws?", I emphasized the importance of a good church. The content of that emphasis has remained largely unchanged through the years and the printing of an estimated 250 million copies of the booklet in every major language. Millions have read the following words of encouragement from the Four Spiritual Laws:

"God's Word admonishes us not to forsake 'the assembling of ourselves together. . . .'[8] Several logs burn brightly together; but put one aside on the cold hearth and the fire goes out. So it is with your relationship to other Christians. If you do not belong to a church, do not wait to be invited. Take the initiative; call the pastor of a nearby church where Christ is honored and His Word is preached. Start this week, and make plans to attend regularly."

The Need for Others

Fellowship is vitally important, for it is almost impossible for one to maintain a vital, warm and personal relationship with the Lord Jesus Christ apart from regular fellowship with other believers who share your love and devotion and enthusiasm for the Savior.

f. Encourage your disciple to be baptized and join a local church. Baptism is a part of one's commitment to Christ which is often overlooked and minimized in the disciple-building process. In the Great Commission, Jesus said, "As you go making disciples, baptize them and teach them." It is very important that believers be baptized as an act of obedience to our Lord's command and as a means of following His example.

g. Emphasize the importance of love. Read the great passages in the Scriptures that emphasize love, especially I Corinthians 13, and ask God to demonstrate that quality in your own life, as an example. As Jesus reminds us in John 13:35, "By this will all men know that you are My disciples, if you have love for one another." As I Corinthians 13 reminds us, no matter what else we might do for God, everything is of no value at all apart from love.

h. Teach your disciple the importance of following the example of the Lord as a servant. Our Lord, though He was God, did not demand and cling to His rights as God, but humbled Himself by dying on the cross for our sins. Every true disciple must learn how to be a servant — following the example of our Lord.

In Campus Crusade, for example, the greater the responsibility, the more we emphasize the qualities of being a servant. As someone has said, "Instead of developing schools for Christian leadership, we should have more schools for Christian servants."

i. Teach your disciples how to be good stewards of their time, talent and treasure. We must never forget that everything we have is a gift from God. The Lord has given Vonette and me the liberty, indeed the admonition, to make a strong emphasis in our ministry on stewardship in every area of life.

Accountability

God does not *need* our time, our talent, our treasure; but man is so created that we do not find fulfillment until we have acknowledged our accountability to God and have obeyed His commands. Help your disciples to understand and obey the spiritual law of sowing and reaping.

j. Finally, impart a vision for the fulfillment of the Great Commission in the minds and hearts of those whom you are seeking to disciple. For example, if your disciple is a student, plan together how he or she can help to evangelize in classes, dorms or other segments of the campus population.

If your disciple is a mother, share with her how she and her husband can win and disciple the couples in their neighborhood for Christ. Or, if you are discipling business executives, show them how they can start Bible studies and evangelistic luncheons to help reach the business community.

Remember, "small plans do not inflame the minds of men." Help your disciples dream great dreams, and as you develop in your relationships with them, teach them the truths of God's Word and concentrate on relating discipleship to their personal strategies for helping to fulfill the Great Commission.

Joy – and Sorrow

You may ask, "What about failures and disappointments?"

There have been many. Often I have shed tears of heartache and sorrow over men and women into whose lives we have poured ourselves with much prayer and time, only to have them drift away to dishonor our Lord. People whom God has honored and whose lives have been fruitful have become like Demas, "having loved this present world," forsaking the Lord.[9] But through it all there has been a reminder of the promise of the Lord Jesus, ". . . Lo, I am with you always."[10]

In the beginning years of the ministry I was especially distressed when some of the choicest young people who had such great promise for the Lord drifted away. I could not understand it. We had prayed for them, we had loved them, we had spent time with them. Then the Lord reminded me that they were His responsibility. He reminded me of the parable of the sower and the soils, and how not all the seed fell on good soil. I learned that I needed to trust God and to continue obeying His command to win and disciple every person possible for Christ.

Perspective on Success

Out of that philosophy, out of that spirit, grew the statement, "Successful witnessing is simply taking the initiative to share Christ in the power of the Holy Spirit and leaving the results to God." And I could easily paraphrase, "Successful disciple-building is simply taking the initiative to build disciples in the power of the Holy Spirit and leaving the results to God."

May I encourage you to begin today to pray that God will give you one or more individuals into whom you can pour your life, helping them to understand how to become disciples and disciplers of others for the glory, honor and praise of our living Lord.

CHAPTER 15

How to Build a Supernatural Church

For more than 30 years I have been committed to the church of Jesus Christ. As previously mentioned, I became a Christian through the influence of the First Presbyterian Church of Hollywood where I was also nourished in my faith as a young believer. Shortly after receiving Christ, I began graduate study at Princeton Theological Seminary and later transferred to Fuller Theological Seminary. I continued my studies for five years while also directing my business in Los Angeles. In 1951 I felt led by the Lord to start Campus Crusade.

Through the years since then, I have had the opportunity to work with many thousands of churches through the ministry of Campus Crusade through Here's Life, America and Here's Life, World. My responsibilities take me to almost every major continent to meet with Christian leaders, pastors, missionaries and others from scores of countries each year. Because of this background, I have learned some valuable lessons.

In my interaction with pastors, literally scores of them have indicated that they were thinking seriously about leaving the ministry. As we have counseled together, I have been able to share certain truths and experiences with them that have not only caused them to remain in the ministry but have also caused them to become excited about the privilege of doing so. In the months and years that have followed, their ministries have been revolutionized.

One pastor had left his church over the protests of his congregation because, as he put it, "I am a defeated person and an ineffective pastor." His congregation loved him and accepted his resignation reluctantly. He came to one of our seminars where he learned how to be controlled and empowered by the Holy Spirit and how to share his faith with others. After three days of meetings, training and fellowship, he came to announce that he was now prepared to go back to his church. "My church is going to have a new pastor," he said, "and I am going to be that pastor."

Essential Ingredients

From my exposure to thousands of pastors, I believe that there are certain things that are essential in building a church that will honor the Lord Jesus Christ, bring blessing and spiritual growth to its members and teach them how to live supernatural lives.

First of all, I believe it's imperative that the pastor be sure of his call. He needs to ask, "Am I involved in the ministry as a vocation or am I genuinely concerned about the spiritual needs of those to whom I minister? Has God really called me to preach? Do I enjoy preaching? Do I enjoy representing the Lord Jesus Christ in the pulpit and among my people?"

Second, the pastor must commit himself to a holy life and to a life of prayer and Bible study.

Third, he must be an example to his people in the area of discipleship and evangelism. If I were a pastor, I would take whatever training was available from those best qualified to teach me, so that I would become able, efficient and fruitful in these areas.

Lead the Leaders

Fourth, the pastor needs to encourage the leadership of the church to join him in weekend retreats where they can spend time getting acquainted, sharing heartfelt needs, praying and asking God to send revival to their own lives, as leaders of the church, as well as to the congregation.

Fifth, if I were a pastor, I would emphasize prayer in every facet of the church program. I would organize a 24-hour chain of prayer, inviting the members to participate in 96 15-minute periods around the clock. They could rotate every 30 days so that different people would be responsible for the difficult hours.

I would teach my people how to pray and would invite volunteers to pray for me each week. I would arrange to meet with a group of seven or so volunteers early Sunday morning each week, and during the course of the week they would pray specifically for me. A similar group would meet with my wife and agree to pray for her. Others would agree to pray for the associate pastor and other members of the staff.

Goal-setting

Sixth, it is important to set both numerical and spiritual goals for church growth. The pastor should not be satisfied with the *status quo* or even the best of human achievement. These goals should require supernatural intervention and the enabling of the Holy Spirit. They should, however, be realistic and obtainable so as not to discourage the leadership and membership of the church. But there should be definite goals.

Seventh, it would be good to select a staff member or lay leader of the church to devote time to administrative responsibilities within the church. This would relieve the pastor from certain tasks that are very important but might interfere with his attention to Bible study, prayer, preaching, teaching and ministering to the spiritual needs of other people.

Eighth, as a pastor, I would encourage all of the membership to be involved in Lay Institutes for Evangelism where they would learn how to live consistent, Spirit-controlled Christian lives and how to share their faith in Christ more effectively with others.

Ninth, I would encourage key laymen who are ready to be discipled to meet with me at least once or twice each week for prayer, for instruction and for training in evangelism and discipleship. Everything I would teach them, they would, in turn, teach others, so that within a year there would be scores of men and women equipped to teach and model basic discipleship and evangelism concepts.

Creative Brainstorming

Tenth, I think it would be very meaningful to have a brainstorming session with the most creative people and to develop the most attractive, creative type of worship service possible. For example, I would train the ushers to be warm, loving and outgoing, so that every person who enters the service would feel wanted, loved and prayed for from the opening hymn of praise to the benediction. I would devote at least 20 minutes to congregational singing, with special emphasis on worship, praise, adoration and thanksgiving to God.

The sermon would be based on Scripture and saturated with the love and praise of God.

I would teach my people the attributes of God so that they would understand that their attitudes, actions and everything about them is influenced by their view of God. I would teach them in such a way that they would be more concerned about what God thinks than with what man thinks. It was said of the Puritans that they feared no one but God. The Christians of today seem to fear everyone but God!

Worship a Priority

Eleventh, I think it would be important to be willing to break with a practice of tradition that inhibits worship of God and praise of Him. I think there should be times, especially in the informal worship hours Sunday evening and Wednesday, when the people would be able to share their victories, their defeats, their heartaches and their sorrows. This should result in their being loved and prayed for by their brothers and sisters in Christ. These times of sharing, however, should be designed to teach people how to trust God rather than to depend on each other as a crutch.

Twelfth, the pastor should warn his people against developing the attitude permeating the church today: "What can I get out of church?" instead of asking, "What can I give?" They need to recognize the truths of the law of God, that the one who seeks happiness never finds it, but the one who lives to help and serve others is the one who finds true fulfillment and meaning in life.

This is the great paradox of the Christian life — before one can truly live, there must be death. This is what the apostle Paul is referring to in Galatians 2:20: "I am crucified with Christ; and it is no longer I who live, but Christ lives in me; and the life which I now live in the flesh I live by faith in the Son of God, who loved me, and delivered Himself up for me." Christ must be Lord of every area. The only fulfilled and happy Christians are those who have surrendered every area of their lives to Christ.

The Importance of Giving

Thirteenth, congregations need to be taught the exciting adventure of giving. God's promise is "whatever a man sows, this he will also reap."[1] I would teach my people to sow generously of their time, talent and material possessions with the assurance that they will always reap more than they sow.

We tend to be very selfish people. God has blessed the United States and Canada with at least 75% of the trained Christian workers and 80% of the evangelical Christian wealth in the world. Yet we represent only six percent of the world's population. "From everyone who has been given much shall much be required."[2]

Fourteenth, I think it is imperative that Christians become "world Christians," helping to fulfill the Great Commission by winning and discipling men of all nations (see Chapter 16).

Home and Family

Fifteenth, I would encourage my members to spend at least one night alone as a family at home and then give suggestions as to how they can maximize that evening, making it the most meaningful through playing games, studying the Scriptures, talking and sharing together. This is of great importance to the health of the family and the vitality of the church.

Sixteenth, a member of the church or a qualified leader should be trained to work with the youth, prisoners in local penal institutions, and older people in hospitals and convalescent homes. Members of a church need to bring great glory to God by their holy lives and fruitful witness. In fact, I now pray this prayer daily for the staff and all who are associated with this ministry.

Collectively, our Christian witness in the world is only as strong as the Body of Christ is healthy. As the church is invigorated by the proper balance of worship, service and each member's concern for the other, we will see God do supernatural, impossible things through our presence in the world.

CHAPTER 16

How to Develop a World Vision

For the past 26 years I have signed my letters, "Yours for fulfilling the Great Commission in this generation." I have tried to weigh my every decision and action in light of the Great Commission of our Lord. It is my strong conviction and commitment that every Christian should prioritize his time, talent and treasure in terms of how he can contribute the most to the fulfillment of the Great Commission.

How can one develop a supernatural "world vision" for Christ and His kingdom? There are 12 keys to becoming a "world Christian" that I would like to share with you. You may wish to communicate these thoughts with those whom you are seeking to disciple.

Recognize God's Sovereignty

I am sometimes asked, "What motivates you to be continually involved in the fulfillment of the Great Commission? How do you keep your heart for evangelism and discipleship aflame for the Lord?" First let me say that I can claim no credit. Such motivation is the result of a sovereign work of God's grace in my heart.

From a human perspective, I have no more concern for the souls of others than anyone else. Basically, all of us — Christians and non-Christians alike — are selfish. We want what we want, when we want it, whether it is convenient for others or not.

However, something wonderful happens when we claim by faith the reality of being crucified and raised with Christ, according to Galatians 2:20 and Romans, chapters six and eight, for example. We actually begin to live the resurrection life of Christ. As a result, we increasingly think the way He thinks and love the way He loves.

As I have already shared, one midnight hour in the spring of 1951, God spoke to me in a sovereign, unique, supernatural way concerning my role in helping to fulfill the Great Commission. The vision embraced the entire world and resulted in the ministry of Campus Crusade.

Sometimes I am asked the question, "Are you surprised at the phenomenal growth and success of Campus Crusade?" My answer is, "No." For according to the original vision, we have only begun to see what God is going to do.

But every Christian has an important role to play in helping to fulfill the Great Commission. You can discover your role by asking God to show you what He wants you to do. Since He is sovereign and rules in the affairs of men and nations, He will show you what He wants you to do if you ask Him and obey what He tells you to do.

Study God's Attributes

If we are to develop a world vision, we must grow in our understanding of the character of God. As I mentioned in the first chapter of this book, everything hinges on our view of God. If we know Him to be the omnipotent, creator God who but spoke and a hundred billion galaxies were flung into space — if we know Him to be the holy, righteous, sovereign, all-wise, all-knowing, all-powerful God — if we know Him to be the loving, compassionate heavenly Father — then we will have no problem surrendering our wills and ways to Him.

In fact, one cannot truly understand the attributes of God without kneeling in reverence with yielded will saying, "Lord, what will You have me to do?" It is not a matter of being coerced into serving the Lord; it is simply a matter of knowing who God is. When we make that glorious discovery, we will gladly serve Him with great joy and gratitude from our innermost being.

To know God is to love Him, and to love Him is to serve Him. As with Isaiah of old and multitudes like him through the centuries, we, too, can say to the Lord, "Here am I. Send me!"[1]

Make a Total Commitment

World vision does not come to all Christians, only to those who have made a total, irrevocable commitment of their lives to the Lord Jesus Christ. God's Word reminds us in Psalms 25:14, "Friendship with God is reserved for those who reverence Him. With them alone He shares the secrets of His promises." God does not share His burden for the world with carnal, disobedient Christians. He only does so with those who are His bondslaves by choice.[2]

The privilege of serving our wonderful Lord as an act of the will has been powerfully described by C. T. Studd, the famous missionary. I agree with his appraisal, "If Christ be God and died for me, there is nothing too great that I can do for Him."[3]

Be Filled With the Spirit

Only those who walk in the fullness and power of the Holy Spirit can be world Christians and help fulfill the Great Commission.

On the eve of His crucifixion Jesus told His disciples, "It is expedient for you that I go away; for if I go not away, the Comforter [the Holy Spirit] will not come unto you. . . . When He, the Spirit of Truth, is come, He will guide you into all truth: for He shall not speak of Himself; but whatsoever He shall hear, that shall He speak: and He will show you things to come. He shall glorify Me."[4]

Forty days after the crucifixion, Jesus commanded His disciples to wait in Jerusalem until they were empowered with the Spirit from on high. Remember that the disciples were defeated, fruitless, spiritually-impotent men, even though they had been with our Lord for three and a half years. Later, at Pentecost, they were filled with the Holy Spirit and went out to turn their world upside down.

Be Accountable to God

God will someday hold each of us accountable for the work He has given us to do. Study Scripture passages that reveal God's love for the lost and our accountability to Him (such as Matthew 25:14-30 and Colossians 1:13,14).

Meditate on Great Commission Passages

From the time we awaken in the morning until we go to bed at night, we should be involved in the fulfillment of the Great Commission. Every attitude, every action, all of our time, talent and treasure should be directed toward this end. Believing that you "have not been called to help fulfill the Great Commission" or that "the standards are too high" *can* be excuses which demonstrate a lack of faith and obedience. God never asks us to do anything that He does not enable us to do.

Jesus has clearly established His standards for disciple-ship. "Anyone who wants to be My follower must love Me far more than he does his own father, mother, wife, children, brothers and sisters — yes, more than his own life — other-wise he cannot be My disciple." Yet, as I have mentioned, when we obey this command of our Lord, He enables us to love our families and everyone else even more. Further, whatever we give up to follow Him will be returned to us a hundredfold.

Study the History of Missions and Movements

Historically, God has raised up special movements to ac-complish certain objectives. In our time and in phenomenal ways, God has formed the Navigators, Inter-Varsity Christian Fellowship, Young Life, Youth for Christ, Far Eastern Gospel Broadcasting, Transworld Radio, HCJB, World Literature Crusade, Wycliffe Bible Translators, Child Evangelism Fel-lowship, Gospel Recordings, the Gideons, Christian Business Men's Committee, Bible Study Fellowship, various women's groups and hundreds of others, including Campus Crusade for Christ, in addition to various denominational groups that are faithful to Him. None of these movements is doing exactly the same thing. God has developed them for unique ministries.

Consider God's sovereign role in raising up such special movements; pray for them; seek out ways in which you can support their ministries. If possible, become actively involved in one of them.

Study the Biographies of Influential Missionaries

Thousands, if not millions, of people have given their lives to help fulfill the Great Commission. The study of those biog-raphies that are available is of great benefit to anyone. Con-sider in particular the lives of such godly missionaries and evangelists as Andrew Murray, C. T. Studd, Hudson Taylor, John R. Mott, Adoniram Judson, "Praying" Hyde, George Whitefield, John Wesley, Charles Finney, and Dwight L. Moody. Find out what motivated these servants to love the Lord "more than their own lives" and to give their lives as "living sacrifices" that they might do their part in helping to fulfill the Great Commission in their time.

Study the World's Need for Christ

Ask various mission movements to supply you with data concerning needs of the world from their perspective. Pray for missions and for missionaries. Secure photographs and names of missionaries in whom you are particularly interested and pray for them daily. The very act of expressing compassion and concern for others will open your heart to the world.

Be Prepared to Go

Do not be afraid to offer *yourself* to God to help fulfill the Great Commission! He is completely worthy of your trust. You can say to Him, "Lord, I will go where You want me to go; I will do what You want me to do; I will say what You want me to say — whatever it costs."

You will never have cause to question or doubt His faithfulness, for His Word reminds us, "The steps of good men are directed by the Lord. He delights in each step they take."[6]

Visit the Mission Field

It is possible on a short-term basis to visit different foreign fields. Why not pray that God will arrange for you to make such a visit? And when you go, do not be afraid to offer yourself to God for service. Experience has proven that a good percentage of those who take short-term missionary assignments in foreign countries return for a lifetime of ministry!

Don't Forget – the Sound Mind Principle

Finally, ask God to show you how to maximize your life for Christ, according to the sound mind principle of Scripture. We are not to wait for impressions or dramatic experiences, though God may speak to you in such a way. We are to use our minds, and we are to obey the Word of God.

There is an inherent danger in looking for emotional or subjective experiences as Christians. God does not usually impress upon us the direction we are to go or the kind of work we are to do apart from the use of our minds.

Our Lord commands us to love God with all of our hearts, souls, minds and strength. To repeat, we are to love God with our minds. Our minds should therefore be controlled by the mind of Christ, because the Scriptures tell us that we actually have a portion of the very mind of Christ.

As we seek to know and to do the will of God, we should analyze our talents, our training, our personal likes and dislikes. As we relate them to the needs of the world and walk in the Spirit, God will show us what He would have us do. There may or may not be an emotional, subjective impression, but He will make known to us His will if only we trust and obey Him.

Join the Here's Life Movement

Whoever you are, wherever you are, God will use you to help change this world if you are available! Again, availability is far more important than ability, though both are important. Changed men in sufficient numbers equal a changed world. Only Jesus Christ can change men, and He chooses to do it through us as Christians. He wants to start now.

The Here's Life movement exists to help Christians evangelize and disciple right where they live. A spiritual awakening throughout the entire world can be accomplished only as millions of Christians commit themselves to Jesus Christ as Lord of their lives and develop personal strategies of discipleship and evangelism that tie in directly with His global strategy. A single Christian controlled and empowered by the Holy Spirit, with a personal strategy, focusing all his efforts on helping to fulfill the Great Commission, can multiply his fruitfulness many times over.

Possibly there is a Here's Life movement in your country or community. Become involved in the Here's Life training. Learn how to live the Spirit-controlled and -empowered life. Learn how to share your faith more effectively with others. Learn how to disciple other Christians to win and disciple still others for our Lord.

Check the local telephone directory for the number and address of Here's Life in your area. If there is no such movement in your area, please contact Here's Life, Arrowhead Springs, San Bernardino, CA 92414 to learn how you can become involved.

Develop a Personal Strategy

A personal strategy is a deliberate plan of action by an individual to accomplish a specific goal. Since the goal of every sincere believer should be to help fulfill the Great

Commission, his personal plan should include evangelizing and discipling, adding and multiplying.

When you personally introduce another to Christ, that is spiritual addition. But when you deliberately disciple the new Christian and help him to win, disciple and send others who will do the same with still others, generation after spiritual generation — that is *spiritual multiplication*.

Beginning with only two persons, and using this simple, continuous cycle of spiritual multiplication, assuming that the process continues unbroken, the entire world could be totally evangelized and saturated with the gospel in less than 32 subsequent steps, because two multiplied by itself 32 times equals more than the population of the world.

The "How-to's"

There are a number of tangible steps you can take, starting now, to put your personal strategy for helping to fulfill the Great Commission into effect.

First, be sure that you are committed to Christ and filled with the Holy Spirit. There are thousands of guilt-ridden, carnal Christians who have become so frustrated and confused that God cannot use them. In each case, there is undoubtedly a lack of faith or trust in God and a lack of obedience in doing His will. Basically, the average Christian often does not trust God to do what He promised to do.

Whatever your situation, you can trust a loving God when you surrender every life ambition to Him. There is no experience in life that compares with seeking first the kingdom of God, keeping Christ in control of our lives, doing what He calls us to do and being instruments through whom He changes lives. This is real living — life at its highest and best.

Ask God for Guidance

Second, pray in faith that God will guide you in developing your personal strategy. Ask God for an effective strategy to reach your immediate area of influence for Christ. You do not have to design your own strategy; you are simply discovering the plan that God has already designed for you.

Jesus gave us a perfect example. While on earth He discussed every major decision and turning point in His life with His heavenly Father. And remember as you pray to expect

God to provide both the strategy and the wisdom to implement it. Expectant faith pleases God.

Third, outline the strategy that God reveals in answer to your prayers. Make lists of specific people with whom you can share Christ. Consider specific groups in your life and develop a strategy to reach each one.

Begin with your family. Remember that in your home, more than any other place, your life will be your testimony. Demonstrate love and avoid preaching or high pressure methods to reach your loved ones. For example, explain to your loved ones that because of Christ, you love and care for them even *more* than before you received Christ. Trust God continually to fill you with His Spirit, so that your actions — the fruit of the Spirit — will bear witness to what Jesus has done in your life.

Plan how to reach the people with whom you study or work. Seek those whom you know to be Christians and ask them to join you in a discipleship group and in sharing Christ with others in your office.

Be Available

In your church, make yourself available to your pastor. Offer to teach Sunday school. Become a part of the visitation and evangelism team. Encourage other members of your church to develop their own personal strategies.

Invite your neighbors for an evangelistic coffee, tea or dessert. Try organizing a neighborhood Bible study. Tell your friends what Christ has done in your life and that He can do the same in theirs.

Pray for those with whom you want to share Christ. Then take the initiative; go to them! Tell them of God's love and forgiveness, available through Jesus Christ. Give them opportunities to receive Him. Share your faith as a way of life and ask God to enable you to talk about Christ with others daily as a way of life.

As others trust Him as Lord and Savior, begin to disciple them and involve them in the cycle of multiplication. Invite them to join you in an effort to saturate your entire community with the message of Christ.

Utilize the mass media — radio, television, newspapers and magazines — to reach every person possible with the good news. Prayerfully investigate opportunities to influence the communications media for Christ and to encourage godly, trustworthy and qualified people to enter public office.

Expand Your Faith

Ask Christ to expand your faith as He reveals His strategy to you, remembering that He has a perfect plan which will enable you to help fulfill the Great Commission in your community.

Fourth, learn everything you can about how to accomplish your personal strategy in helping to fulfill the Great Commission. Take advantage of special training and materials offered by Campus Crusade and various other Christian organizations and churches to learn techniques of sharing Christ more effectively with others. Learn how to build other Christians in their faith and help send them forth to the world with the good news of God's love and forgiveness.

May I encourage you to write out your personal strategy today? List others with whom God has impressed you to share Christ. Then begin immediately to work out your strategy to share your faith with them.

Just as an example, there are over 250,000 international students studying in the United States from nearly every country in the world. These students are generally more open to the gospel than they are in their home countries. Further, they usually represent the potential leadership of the countries from which they have come.

A Ministry for Everyone

There tends to be a feeling that ministry to international students is the responsibility of some small group of "specialists." Nothing could be further from the truth! One of the most strategic investments that any of us can make is to help win and disciple international students for the Savior, so that when they return to their various countries, they can be powerful witnesses for Him, as so many already are.

In addition to personal ministry, invest your resources in world evangelism and discipleship. Jesus Himself said that where our treasure is, there will our hearts be also. One of the best ways to remind yourself continually of the world's need for Christ is to begin investing your resources in this regard.

You will find your interest will immediately grow, you will pray more often for that interest, and you will find yourself becoming more sensitive to world needs.

If you desire to commit yourself to help fulfill His Great Commission, why not make the following prayer your own:

"Dear Father in heaven, I stand at attention. I make myself available to You to do with me as You wish. I want to be one of Your ambassadors through whom You can bring Your message of love and forgiveness in Christ to all people everywhere. I invite You to cleanse me, to empower me, to lead me, to inspire me, to teach me, to enable me to do that which will bring the greatest honor and glory to Your name. Anoint me by Your Holy Spirit to contribute my maximum to the fulfillment of the Great Commission in my time. I ask this in the name of Jesus. Amen."

If this prayer expresses the desire of your heart and you would like additional information as to how you can help to fulfill the Great Commission, please write to me.

CHAPTER SEVENTEEN

Fulfilling the Great Commission by the End of 1980

Jesus told His disciples, "I have been given all authority in heaven and earth. Therefore go and make disciples in all the nations, baptizing them into the name of the Father and of the Son and of the Holy Spirit, and then teach these new disciples to obey all the commands I have given you; and be sure of this — that I am with you always, even to the end of the world."[1]

For centuries, the stirring command of our Lord as recorded in Matthew 28 has served as the banner for an army of love. Untold numbers of believers throughout the history of the Christian era have joined ranks in obedience to these words. Their objective — the fulfillment of the Great Commission.

Today, the inspiring force of those words has martialed an imposing contingent of Christians who share in the vision of their forebears. I trust that you are among them.

As you are praying for and taking advantage of your opportunities to tell others the most joyful news ever announced — the gospel of our Lord — then you, too, are a member of the King's host. And today, you have the unprecedented privilege of witnessing the fulfillment of His royal directive.

Not Just America, but the World

For many years the staff and friends of Campus Crusade, a tiny part of God's vast legion, have prayed and worked for the fulfillment of our Lord's Great Commission by the target dates of 1976 in the United States and 1980 in the world. Today, we firmly believe that God, working through many movements, men and means, has honored the first of these prayers with the *initial fulfillment* of the Great Commission in the U.S. by the end of 1976. Now we are more convinced than ever that the entire world will be reached with the gospel by the end of 1980.

Yet we also realize that the magnitude of this claim re-
quires an explicit definition. What do we mean by "the Great
Commission"? What do we mean by "initial fulfillment"?
Must the entire world be Christianized before the Great
Commission can be considered to have been fulfilled?

The answers to these questions are found in the words of
our Lord Himself.

His Command

The Great Commission of our Lord, as expressed in
Matthew 28:18,19 and in Mark 16:15, is a command to His
followers to take the gospel to every nation, making disciples
in the process. We define "nations" to include cultures, tribes
and languages within the more than 210 countries and protectorates throughout the world.

You will notice that these two passages contain both a
qualitative and a *quantitative* aspect. Matthew 28 commands
us to "make disciples of all the nations . . . baptizing . . . and
teaching them" (qualitative), while Mark 16 proclaims that
we are to "preach the Good News to everyone everywhere"
(quantitative).

But the question arises, does the Great Commission
specify in these verses a distinction between preaching the
gospel (evangelizing) and making disciples (discipling)? And
if so, would that mean that the Great Commission could not be
fulfilled in any area until all Christians were mature believers? The answer is "No!"

Evangelism and Discipleship

As we have seen in a previous chapter, "disciple" is a term
which describes simply a "follower of the Lord Jesus Christ."
There is no biblical basis on which to assume that such a
believer will be a "committed" or a "mature" Christian.

Most leading Bible scholars agree that the Greek word for
"disciple," *mathetes,* does not describe a particularly advanced
state of Christian maturity but rather a basic relationship to
Christ.

A careful reading of Matthew 28:18-20 does not demand
that every community have a core of "committed" disciples
before the Great Commision can be fulfilled. Though the
passage does demand the existence of disciples, it does not

indicate whether they are to be "committed" or "believer" disciples.

The New Testament references to disciples includes both those who are believers who have received Jesus Christ as their Savior but may still be carnal or "believer disciples" and those who have forsaken all to follow Christ — "committed disciples."

We are praying that by the end of 1980 there will be large numbers of "believer disciples" in every country of the world as a result of present and planned evangelistic thrusts in those countries. These believers may be young and untaught, but if they have truly accepted Christ as Savior and Lord, we believe they "fit" the biblical standard given in the Great Commission passages.

Continuing Priority

Some Christians ask, "Is our responsibility fulfilled when a number of believers have been established in a given 'nation,' 'tribe,' or 'culture'? Will the Great Commission, once fulfilled, cease to be a priority?" Indeed not!

Evangelism and the process of making disciples is to be a present, continuous, ongoing privilege for the Christian — a privilege that will not cease until our Lord Himself returns.

As we previously discussed, Paul was not satisfied with just "talking about Christ to all who would listen." He wanted to assist them in their Christian growth until they became mature, "committed disciples."

So, having initially fulfilled the Great Commission in any country does not mean that there is nothing more to do. The fact is, the challenge is even greater. Millions of "young" Christians, including those who have been Christians for many years without evidencing any significant spiritual growth, will need to be discipled, continually nurtured and instructed.

Initial Fulfillment

There is an initial evangelization that must first occur in an area before the ongoing process of nurturing disciples can begin to accelerate, though in a very real sense, they are simultaneous and cannot be separated. True discipling of Christians involves evangelism, and true evangelism involves discipling of believers. Once this initial evangelization has been accomplished in a given area, the Great Commission in that area can be said to have been initially fulfilled.

What conditions will accompany that fulfillment? How many will have had to hear the gospel message before this initial fulfillment can be assumed to have taken place? Let us see what the Scriptures have to say.

The apostle Paul wrote to the church in Thessalonica, "For the word of the Lord has sounded forth from you, not only in Macedonia and Achaia, but also in every place your faith toward God has gone forth, so that we have no need to say anything."[2]

Paul seems to be saying that wherever he goes throughout Macedonia and Achaia, he finds that the gospel and the testimony of the Thessalonians has preceded him. In other words, widespread evangelization had occurred to such an extent that the apostle Paul apparently could find no one who had not already heard the gospel message in this area.

The Holy Spirit inspired Luke to record the account of Paul's preaching in Ephesus: "And this took place for two years, so that all who lived in Asia [Asia Minor] heard the word of the Lord, both Jews and Greeks."[3] This verse *does not* necessarily mean that *every single person* in Asia Minor had been *personally* confronted with the gospel through Paul's witness. However, it does seem to indicate that the area was evangelized in an overall sense and that directly and indirectly everyone had had an opportunity to receive Christ.

Most Will Have Heard

Therefore, in light of God's inspired Word, we may set forth a definition of the initial fulfillment of the Great Commission. It is the preaching and sharing of the gospel to such an extent that the percentage of those who are *known* to have heard it will be sufficiently great as to suggest that the rest of the nation has also heard the message, either from primary or secondary sources.

But what will characterize the individual and the society in regions where the Great Commission has been initially fulfilled? Certainly, there are aspects of American society that belie what we believe to have already taken place by the end of 1976.

For example, the crime rate continues to be a major concern for most Americans. In addition, issues such as homosexual rights and abortion now command public debate while moral absolutes wane. And certainly there are still many closed and spiritually cold hearts today. If the Great Commission has been initially fulfilled here, why do such conditions exist?

Satanic Counterattack

Such a question assumes that a spiritual utopia will follow on the heels of the fulfillment of the Great Commission in a given community or country. But such is not, nor has it ever been, the case. There will be no idyllic spiritual climate prior to our Lord's glorious return. Do not forget that our adversary, Satan himself, is waging a spiritual counterattack against the inroads that the Spirit of God is making in the world.

Do not forget the words of the apostle Paul in I Corinthians 2:14, "But a natural man does not accept the things of the Spirit of God, for they are foolishness to him, and he cannot understand them, because they are spiritually appraised."

"Natural" men are blind to spiritual truths. Not all men will respond positively to the gospel even though they *hear* it. Multitudes will tragically tread the path leading to destruction. And our society today clearly bears their depraved imprint.

Yet, a moral and spiritual awakening has swept America as the result of millions of Christians claiming for their country God's promise to Solomon in II Chronicles 7:14, that if people will humble themselves, confess their sins and pray, He will forgive and heal.

The Gospel — Heard Everywhere

By 1976, the media was carrying the gospel at a rate unmatched by any other time in history. According to the National Religious Broadcasters, by the end of 1976, 125 million people were being ministered to each week over radio and television by such men as Billy Graham, Theodore Epp, Oral Roberts, Rex Humbard, Pat Robertson, Jerry Falwell, Robert Schuller, Richard De Haan and hundreds of others.

In addition, God used Campus Crusade in a unique way through Here's Life, America. We were privileged to work with approximately 15,000 churches of all denominations in 246 major cities and thousands of smaller communities throughout the nation to help train 325,000 Christians in communicating the gospel. In turn, these trained believers then influenced millions for Christ. Our marketing consultant estimated that 175 million people were exposed to the "I found it!" campaign — one of the most significant thrusts of Here's Life, America.

In the light of all these signs, we believe that we have an abundance of evidence that indicates that the Great Commission has been initially fulfilled in the United States. And we believe that what has happened here, through grace and the enabling power of the Holy Spirit, will in considerable measure occur on a worldwide scale by the end of 1980.

To the World by 1980

This does not mean that by the end of 1980 every country will be "Christianized" or even that a majority of its people will become Christians. But it does mean that everyone who has the ability to comprehend will have had a chance to hear the gospel.

By faith we in the ministry of Campus Crusade are "believing God for the impossible." In addition to our basic ministries, we are launching a number of bold new thrusts in evangelism and discipleship which we believe have, through the enabling of the Holy Spirit, the potential of helping to introduce at least one billion people to Christ during the next 10 years.

These strategies are and will be carried out in cooperation with millions of trained Christians from thousands of local churches of all denominations and hundreds of other Christian organizations throughout the world.

These will include:

1. *The expansion of Here's Life campaigns to thousands of additional cities throughout the world.* Already many millions are being reached for Christ through Here's Life methods of city-, state- and nation-wide saturation campaigns, such as those in South Korea, Colombia and Kerala, South India.

2. *The launching of daily worldwide radio programs in approximately one hundred languages.* These programs will emphasize discipleship and strategy for total saturation of

communities and countries with the gospel. They will utilize long, medium and shortwave broadcasting which will blanket every community in every country of the world.

3. *Training centers,* which have already been established in many countries on every continent. Now we are expanding, as God enables us, to every city above 50,000 population where it is possible to do so in the world. The emphasis will be on discipleship and evangelism and will be directed by national pastors and laymen who share our concern for the fulfillment of the Great Commission. There are more than 2,000 cities in the free world where we are prayerfully planning to start training centers.

4. *Rural Evangelism.* A revolutionary concept of rural evangelism has been developed by our staff in Kenya, Africa, which is designed to develop and depend on national leadership. This phenomenally fruitful concept is already spreading to other countries and continents. We expect many millions to be reached for Christ through this remarkable approach.

5. *Film Ministry.* Campus Crusade, through the generosity of a friend, recently arranged the financing of a film on the life of Jesus, based on the Gospel of Luke. The film was directed by the noted film producer-director John Heyman, founder of the Genesis Project, and will be distributed by Warner Brothers.

In addition to showing the film "Jesus" in thousands of theaters and on worldwide television, we will saturate the rural areas of all developing nations. The film will be available for showing beginning in the fall of 1979, and will ultimately be translated into approximately 150 languages of the world. We prayerfully project that more than two billion people will see this film within the next 10 years, with hundreds of millions responding to the invitation of accepting salvation through Jesus Christ.

Again, I must emphasize that the widespread proclamation of the gospel is only the beginning. We must not stop there! We must continue with the objective of giving every person possible an opportunity to receive Christ through a personal presentation of the gospel and then seek to enlist each one in the local, visible Body of believers — the church — where they will be taught and encouraged to grow to maturity in their Christian faith.

The Great Commission — an impossible, unattainable goal? Humanly speaking, yes. Yet, I am confident that God is going to do something incredibly great to demonstrate His love and forgiveness to all men and nations throughout the world by the end of 1980.

I trust that you are asking, "How can I get involved?" Begin where you are. What are the personal "faith barriers" confronting you right now? Entrust them to the King of kings and Lord of lords. Then claim the treasure chest of His promises to you in the Scriptures.

And be ready to serve on the front lines of this adventure wherever you may be. You can start today by inviting others to join with you in daily or weekly prayer for a spiritual awakening to come to your community, our nation and the entire world. There are many lay, student and pastor's training programs available in most countries and many cities of the free world.

The incredible privilege to be used of God to help bring tens of millions of people to our Savior and Lord will undoubtedly make these next few years the most challenging, demanding and exciting in all of history!

CHAPTER EIGHTEEN

Postscript: Supernaturally Trusting God for the Impossible Beyond 1980

The challenge of helping to reach the world for the Lord Jesus Christ by the end of 1980 is only the beginning of the task which lies ahead for committed disciples with a world vision. We already have a good picture of what happens when a nation is saturated by the gospel: as is the case in America. Millions have made decisions for Christ, but many do not have assurance of their salvation. Most people do not understand the person and ministry of the Holy Spirit and are, therefore, not Spirit-filled. Most do not know how to pray, how to study the Scriptures for spiritual warfare and growth, or how to witness for our Lord Jesus Christ. And so, they need help.

When the whole world has been saturated with the gospel, hundreds of millions will need the same spiritual nurture. They will need to be taught how to walk in the fullness of the Spirit and how to share their faith in Christ with others. They will need training in how to study God's Word so that they can become a part of the ongoing process of helping to fulfill the Great Commission in their generation. At the same time programs of personal and mass evangelism will continue as in America.

Worldwide Revival

America is far from a utopia, but God is doing something unique and revolutionary in our country. I believe that the spiritual awakening which is now increasingly evident in America will continue to sweep the world through 1980 and beyond.

History Provides a Clue

What are some of the changes that we can expect will take place as a result of this worldwide revival? For the answer, we need to look at history.

A great spiritual revival came to England through the ministries of John Wesley, George Whitefield and others during the early and middle part of the 18th century. In the years which followed, a number of social reforms swept England as a direct result of the revival. Women achieved suffrage, child labor laws were enacted, the Salvation Army and other similar organizations were launched, and numerous orphanages were established. William Wilberforce, a committed Christian, influenced by John Wesley, headed the drive that abolished slavery in England. A great missionary enterprise, which included the ministries of Hudson Taylor, C. T. Studd and hundreds of other missionary leaders, was launched from England. This missionary movement directly contributed to the establishment of some 90% of all the schools now existing in the developing countries of the world.

Another example of great awakening is that of the Welsh revival in 1904. Crime was so greatly diminished that the magistrates in certain cities were presented with white gloves, signifying that there were no cases to try. Drunkenness was so dramatically reduced that a wave of bankruptcy swept the taverns of the principalities. Profanity was curbed until it was said that the mules in the coal mines could not understand their orders.

In our own country the preaching of George Whitefield, a contemporary of John Wesley, influenced the lives of many of our nation's forefathers, including some of the skeptics like Benjamin Franklin. As a result, many of the decisions which helped to give birth to our nation began in the context of a spiritual awakening.

The Four States of Revival

According to Dr. J. Edwin Orr, noted writer and authority on revival, there are four main stages through which all great awakenings go. First, there is *personal revival:* Christians establish right relationships with God and begin to exhibit great zeal. Second, there is an *evangelistic movement:* an area becomes saturated with the gospel. Third, *missionary movements* result. And fourth, *social reforms* follow the initial revival by approximately 10 years. Then, after a period of time — years or decades — there is a cooling of zeal among the

Christians, and God finds it necessary to send another spiritual awakening.

I believe that we can expect all of these phases to take place within the next 10 to 25 years. And, as we continue to see the acceleration of all that we are now seeing, we need to remember that we are faced with an enemy.

In Matthew 24, we read our Lord's prediction concerning Satan's attempt to destroy the church: "Then you will be tortured and killed and hated all over the world because you are Mine, and many of you shall fall back into sin and betray and hate each other. And many false prophets will appear and lead many astray. Sin will be rampant everywhere and will cool the love of many. But those enduring to the end shall be saved. "And the Good News about the Kingdom will be preached throughout the whole world, so that all nations will hear it, and then, finally, the end will come."[1]

Our Lord's prophetic warnings suggest to me that the gospel will continue to accelerate throughout America while, at the same time, evil will accelerate as well. I believe that we will see a dramatic change in the media. I believe that Christians are going to demand a moral detergent to eliminate some of the pornographic films that poison the minds of our young people. At the same time, I believe that there will be an acceleration of pressure from anti-God forces.

I believe that there will be a tremendous bridge-building process among all races — Indians, blacks, whites and Hispanic groups. I believe that there will be a more cooperative effort between capital and labor, and more ties of Christian love established among governmental leaders. I believe that every facet of society will be influenced for good because of the present revival that has already begun in our country and is now beginning to sweep the world.

A Dangerous "Religion"

I think that there will be a growing awareness of the evil of our present educational system and that remedial action will be taken.

The whole educational system in our country was originally Christian, born in the church. The Bible was the basic textbook. More than 100 of the first great universities were established as a result of dedicated men and women who loved

Jesus Christ: Harvard, Princeton, Dartmouth, Columbia, Yale — all of these and most of the others had their birth through the Christian church.

But today secular humanism is the religion of the public school. As a policy, God is no longer honored or even acknowledged in the classroom. There is a very strong, well-orchestrated plan on the part of those who have administrative control of education to keep Christ and the Christian influence out of our schools. This is often done on the claim that any Christian emphasis in secular education violates the U. S. Constitution, which insists on separation of church and state.

Most people, even Christians, fail to understand that our Founding Fathers were, for the most part, very religious men. Many of them were Christians. They were not insisting on separation of God and state, but separation of church and state. They sought to avoid duplication in our country of particular sectarian views of the church which had had a negative influence in various countries of Europe. They were seeking to avoid a repetition of that from which our Pilgrim fathers had escaped to the religious freedom of America.

A Heritage of Faith

It is incongruous, but some would have us believe that our Founding Fathers were opposed to our Judeo-Christian heritage. Nothing could be farther from the truth. For example, historians tell us that George Washington, the father of our country, began and ended every day on his knees before an open Bible, reading and praying. These founders recognized the sovereignty of God in the affairs of men and nations and so indicated in the writing of our Constitution. They established the practice of all public officials swearing by the Bible when they take office, the offering of prayers at the beginning of all state and national legislative sessions and many other expressions of belief in God.

However, in our schools today our students are being brainwashed to reject the true God and to worship the "god of Baal," the god of secular humanism. We must recognize that this condition is not going to disappear by itself. Urgent and immediate action is required by knowledgeable and dedicated Christians and other concerned citizens.

The Thomas Jefferson Research Center recently reported that "90% of our educational system in 1776 was moral and spiritual" — based upon the Bible, God's holy and inspired Word. But the report further reveals that "by 1925 the moral and spiritual content had been reduced to 6%, and by 1976 it was no longer measurable."

Since the Christian ethic is the very basis of our culture, this dramatic trend away from the scriptural basis of our curriculum has stricken our nation with a moral cancer which threatens our very survival. Is it any wonder that our nation is becoming increasingly bankrupt, morally and spiritually, and that this spiritual bankruptcy is resulting in all kinds of social, economic and political problems?

Perspective on the Future

There are two extreme views prevalent today concerning the future of the world. On the one hand, there are those who believe that a great awakening that will solve all of our problems will sweep the world. They believe that the millennium will be established and that peace will come to the earth before our Lord returns.

On the other hand, there are those who believe that our Lord's return is imminent. In the meantime, evil will increase across the world and there is nothing that we can do to change or correct these satanic influences. There is a tendency to give up and allow evil to triumph by default. Such a view of Scripture ignores our Lord's commands to go and make disciples of all nations and preach the gospel to all men everywhere.

I believe that both extremes are wrong. God has already demonstrated His supernatural power in life-changing and history-changing events in our time, and I believe that He has only begun to demonstrate His power and love. Remember, "For God so loved the world, that He gave His only begotten Son, that whosoever believeth in Him should not perish, but have everlasting life.[2] It is God's will that no one should perish.[3] So He has even delayed His return in order that more people will have a chance to hear the gospel.

Christ warns us not to set prophetic timetables for His return, for "with the Lord one day is as a thousand years, and a thousand years as one day."[4] No one knows when Christ will return, though we should live holy lives in preparation for His return, as if it might be tomorrow.

We must continue to emphasize evangelism and discipleship, both at home and overseas. Literally hundreds of millions are waiting to receive the Lord; and they, along with the millions who have become Christians in the past few years, need to be discipled so that they can join with us in helping to win and disciple still others for our Lord.

Spiritual Harvest Time

Current surveys indicate that, around the world, at least one out of two who are not already Christians are ready to receive Christ. In Asia, Africa and Latin America, that figure often runs as high as 90%, while in Europe the percentage is much lower — one out of 10 or more. In the United States, the ratio is approximately one out of four. So our goal must be to use every possible means of manpower, money and technology to get the message of salvation out to the world while the field is still white unto harvest. As we continue to trust and obey our Lord, not just until 1980, but through 2000 A.D. and beyond, God will allow us to be a part of the greatest spiritual harvest in the history of mankind.

I recently had the opportunity for an in-depth discussion with a good friend and Christian brother, Dr. Charles Malik, one of the leading statesmen of our time. As one of the founders of the United Nations, and at different times president of all five major bodies within the United Nations, including president of the General Assembly, Dr. Malik freely shares his convictions that Jesus Christ is the only hope for civilization. He is a Christian who has made Christ the Lord of his life and who has learned to seek first the kingdom of God and His righteousness.

Eternal Values

When I thanked Dr. Malik for his example to me as a faithful witness for Christ, he responded by saying, "I am sobered by the words of my Lord, 'Everyone therefore who shall confess Me before men, I will also confess him before My Father who is in heaven. But whoever shall deny Me before men, I will also deny him before My Father who is in heaven.' "⁵

As we talked together about God's plan for men and nations, we both agreed that the most famous, wealthy and powerful in the world are soon forgotten, and little that they do during their brief sojourn on earth is long remembered apart from their contribution to the spiritual welfare of mankind. There can be no question that only what is done for Christ and His kingdom lasts for all eternity.

Total Dedication

In 1903, Lenin started communism with 17 people. In 1917, he took over Russia with only 40,000 followers. Today communists control more than one-third of the world's population, and most of the rest of the world has been influenced and infiltrated by them.

Why have the communists been so successful? Because of their dedication and because they have a definite strategy, a plan of action, to take the world for communism. They have responded to the challenge and are willing to pay the price of personal sacrifice to achieve their goals.

Such was the dedication of the disciples and other first-century Christians. Such has been the dedication of every servant of God who has made any significant impact for Christ and His kingdom through the centuries.

We, however, must not merely match their commitment — we must exceed it! God is looking for disciplined soldiers of the cross — completely committed Christians through whom He can accomplish mighty exploits for His kingdom and fulfill the commission which our Lord gave 2,000 years ago.

Maximizing Our Potential

If the Great Commission is to be fulfilled by 1980 and continue to be fulfilled by each successive generation, Christians in North America must play a major role through the investment of their money, manpower and technology. Furthermore, we have the most advanced technology available to man for communicating the gospel of the Lord Jesus Christ. God has uniquely blessed our nations, not for our own selfish indulgences, but that we might share the great spiritual and material blessings of heaven's bounties with other nations of the world. In addition, we need to invest *ourselves* and go from North America by the tens of thousands to assist our brothers and sisters in the rest of the 210 countries and protectorates of the world to help fulfill the Great Commission.

In I Samuel 14, we read that the army of Israel was paralyzed with fear as they were faced with an overwhelming force of hundreds of thousands of Philistines. But Jonathan, with his bodyguard, decided to go out against the enemy: "Let's go across to those heathen.... Perhaps the Lord will do a miracle for us. For it makes no difference to Him how many enemy troops there are!"[6]

God honored Jonathan's faith and gave victory that day to Israel against overwhelming odds.

Only God Is Able

We look at a world of more than four billion, 500 million people, and we are reminded that the God who created the heavens and the earth and to whom the nations are but a speck in the universe is not overwhelmed by the Herculean assignment of reaching these billions of people with the gospel. It is we who are overwhelmed. Our Lord is the God of miracles; He is the God of the impossible. It is He who has commanded us to go and who has promised to go with us. He is waiting to do for us what He did for Jonathan if only we will trust and obey Him as Jonathan did.

When I grasp the magnitude of God's great plan and the incredible privilege of belonging to Him, I am overwhelmed with joy to think that I am alive in the most dramatic, exciting and fruitful spiritual harvest in history. God has given to our generation the technology, the manpower and the money to reach out to mankind with the "most joyful news ever announced."

As I think about this great privilege, I want to shout to all those throughout the world who do not know our Lord, "Come to Christ and experience His supernatural love and forgiveness, and be assured of a life of purpose, peace, meaning and joy — of eternal life."

I want to encourage all Christians to believe God for the impossible, to help fulfill the Great Commission now while the spiritual harvest is so ripe; to invest of yourselves totally and completely — your time, talent and treasure — to help change the world.

This is your challenge to a New Testament life-style — a call to supernatural living.

185

Footnotes

INTRODUCTION

1. Matthew 5:13,14.
2. J. B. Phillips, *Letters to Young Churches,* The Macmillan Co. 1960, p. xiii.

CHAPTER ONE

1. John 10:10.
2. John 14:12.
3. John 14:14.
4. A. W. Tozer, *The Knowledge of the Holy,* Harper and Row, New York, New York, 1961, p. 9.
5. Psalms 139:7-10.
6. Isaiah 40:30 (LB).
7. Psalms 1:1-6 (LB).
8. Acts 4:24-28 (LB).

CHAPTER TWO

1. Prof. James Stewart, *The Strong Name,* T. and T. Clark, Edinburgh, 1940, p. 78.
2. Ephesians 1:4 (LB).
3. Micah 5:2 (LB).
4. Matthew 2:5,6 (KJV).
5. Hebrews 1:1-3 (LB).
6. Isaiah 7:14 (LB).
7. Matthew 1:18-25 (LB).
8. Hebrews 4:15 (LB).
9. Ephesians 1:9,10 (Phillips).
10. John 7:46 (RSV).
11. John 6:28,29 (KJV).
12. Ephesians 2:8.
13. Matthew 22:38-40 (LB).
14. Matthew 5:43-48.
15. John 13:34,35
16. Mark 7:37
17. Matthew 14:31.
18. Romans 3:23.
19. Romans 6:23.
20. Acts 4:12 (RSV).
21. John 2:19.
22. Romans 5:8.
23. John 14:27 (RSV).
24. Philippians 4:13.
25. Psalms 37:23 (LB).

26. John 10:10.
27. I John 5:11,12.
28. I John 4:18a (KJV).
29. Romans 8:39.
30. Romans 5:8.
31. Matthew 11:28,30.
32. Matthew 12:30.
33. Matthew 10:32,33 (KJV).
34. Revelation 3:20.
35. Hebrews 13:5.

CHAPTER THREE

1. John 14:12-14 (LB).
2. Matthew 28:18.
3. Colossians 1:15,16 (Phillips).
4. Colossians 1:13,14 (LB).
5. Colossians 3:1-3 (LB).
6. Philippians 2:15,16 (LB).
7. II Corinthians 5:17 (KJV).
8. Romans 12:1,2 (LB).
9. Romans 12:1,2 (Phillips).
10. Romans 1:18-32 (LB).
11. I John 2:15-17 (LB).
12. Matthew 6:24,25, 28,29 (LB).
13. Matthew 6:33 (KJV).
14. Matthew 6:33 (LB).
15. Psalms 37:25 (LB),.
16. Philippians 3:4-6 (LB).
17. Romans 3:20-24 (LB).
18. Romans 7:15-23a (LB).
19. Romans 8:1-4 (LB).
20. Romans 1:17 (KJV).
21. Hebrews 11:6.
22. Galatians 3:10,11.
23. Proverbs 4:23b.
24. Proverbs 24:7a (KJV).
25. Colossians 3:5-17 (selected) (LB).

CHAPTER FOUR

1. Proverbs 23:7 (KJV).
2. I Corinthians 2:16 (LB).
3. Luke 19:10.
4. James 1:5-7 (LB).
5. Philippians 4:4-9 (LB).
6. Psalms 25:14 (LB).

7. I John 5:14,15.
8. John 3:16.
9. II Peter 3:9.
10. John 14:13,14.
11. Matthew 28:19,20.
12. Matthew 9:29 (KJV).
13. Galatians 2:20 (LB).
14. Romans 10:17 (KJV).
15. Ephesians 2:8.
16. Philippians 2:13 (KJV).
17. Philippians 4:13 (LB).
18. Hebrews 11:6.

CHAPTER FIVE

1. II Corinthians 5:17 (KJV).
2. II Corinthians 2:14,15.
3. I Corinthians 2:16 (LB).
4. I Corinthians 1:12,13 (LB).
5. I John 2:3 (LB).
6. John 15:20b (LB).
7. Matthew 16:18 (LB).
8. Romans 7:25 (LB).

CHAPTER SIX

1. Matthew 17:21 (LB).
2. Revelation 2:4.
3. Revelation 3:15,16 (LB).
4. Luke 19:10.
5. Mark 10:45.
6. Hebrews 10:9-14,17.
7. Romans 5:20-6:4 (LB).
8. I John 2:3,4 (LB).
9. I John 3:9 (LB).
10. Psalms 138:23,24 (LB).
11. Psalms 32:1-6 (LB).
12. Psalms 51:10-13.
13. Psalms 32:6.
14. James 1:2-4 (LB).

CHAPTER SEVEN

1. John 16:7-14 (LB).
2. Acts 1:5,8 (LB).
3. Ephesians 4:5 (LB).
4. Acts 2:4.
5. Acts 4:8.
6. Acts 4:31.
7. John 3:8 (LB).
8. Galatians 5:22,23 (KJV).
9. Romans 8:26 (KJV).
10. Ephesians 5:18-20.

11. I John 5:14,15.
12. Galatians 5:16-18.
13. Matthew 5:6.
14. Romans 12:1,2 (LB).

CHAPTER EIGHT

1. Galatians 3:11 (KJV).
2. Romans 14:23.

CHAPTER NINE

1. John 3:16 (KJV).
2. John 13:34.
3. I Corinthians 13:4-7 (LB).
4. I John 4:19 (KJV).
5. Romans 5:8 (RSV).
6. John 17:23.
7. Matthew 22:36-40;
   Mark 5:41-48.
8. John 13:34,35.
9. John 15:12.
10. I Corinthians 13:1-3 (LB).

CHAPTER TEN

1. Matthew 6:33.
2. Matthew 6:20.
3. Ephesians 3:20.
4. Malachi 3:8-10 (LB).
5. Matthew 6:19-21,24 (LB).
6. Matthew 6:25-28.
7. I Corinthians 12:4.
8. I Corinthians 12:7 (LB).
9. Deuteronomy 8:18 (LB).
10. Haggai 1:9,10 (LB).
11. I Timothy 5:8 (KJV).
12. Matthew 6:32.
13. Matthew 19:29 (LB).
14. II Corinthians 9:7.
15. I John 4:4 (KJV).

CHAPTER ELEVEN

1. II Timothy 1:7 (KJV).
2. Romans 12:1,2 (LB).
3. John 14:21.
4. James 1:5-7.
5. I John 5:14,15
   (Amplified Bible).
6. Luke 19:10.
7. John 15:8 (LB).
8. Psalms 37:23 (KJV).
9. Colossians 2:6 (KJV).

10. Romans 14:23.
11. Romans 1:17; Hebrews 10:38.
12. Hebrews 11:6.
13. Proverbs 3:5,6 (KJV).
14. II Corinthians 11:14.

CHAPTER TWELVE

1. Revelation 19:1,3,4-6 (LB).
2. Psalms 146:1,2 (LB).
3. Psalms 103:1-6,8,10,13, 17,18 (LB).
4. Psalms 103:22.
5. Isaiah 61:11 (LB).
6. Psalms 33:1-4 (LB).
7. Psalms 145:4.
8. II Chronicles 20:12 (LB).
9. II Chronicles 20:20 (LB).
10. II Chronicles 20:21,22,26.
11. St. Augustine, *Confessions.*
12. James 4:2.
13. Romans 8:26 (KJV).
14. Psalms 42:4,5 (LB).
15. Philippians 4:4.

CHAPTER THIRTEEN

1. John 14:27.
2. Matthew 11:28.
3. I Thessalonians 5:18.
4. Ephesians 5:19-20 (LB).
5. I Peter 5:7 (LB).
6. Matthew 11:30.
7. James 1:2-8 (LB).

CHAPTER FOURTEEN

1. Matthew 28:20 (LB).
2. Colossians 1:28 (LB).
3. II Timothy 2:2 (LB).
4. Matthew 4:19.
5. Acts 1:8.
6. John 14:21.
7. Ephesians 1:17,18 (LB).
8. Hebrews 10:25.
9. II Timothy 4:10.
10. Matthew 28:20.

CHAPTER FIFTEEN

1. Galatians 6:7.
2. Luke 12:48.

CHAPTER SIXTEEN

1. Isaiah 6:8.
2. Romans 1:1; Ephesians 3:1.
3. Norman Grubb, *C. T. Studd: Cricketeer and Pioneer,* Christian Literature Crusade, Fort Washington, Penn., 1972, p. 145.
4. John 16:6,7;13,14 (KJV).
5. Luke 14:26 (LB).
6. Psalms 37:23 (LB).

CHAPTER SEVENTEEN

1. Matthew 28:18-20 (LB).
2. I Thessalonians 1:8.
3. Acts 19:10.

CHAPTER EIGHTEEN

1. Matthew 24:9-14 (LB).
2. John 3:16.
3. II Peter 3:9,15 (LB).
4. II Peter 3:8.
5. Matthew 10:32,33.
6. I Samuel 14:6 (LB).